THE AUSTRALIAN
Women's Weekly

MEDITERRANEAN

THE AUSTRALIAN **Women's Weekly**

MEDITERRANEAN

FRESH, HEALTHY
EVERYDAY RECIPES

Project Editor Emma Hill
Project Designer Alison Shackleton
Editorial Assistant Kiron Gill
Jacket Designer Alison Donovan
Jackets Coordinator Lucy Philpott
Production Editor David Almond
Senior Producer Luca Bazzoli
Creative Technical Support Sonia Charbonnier
Managing Editor Dawn Henderson
Managing Art Editor Alison Donovan
Art Director Maxine Pedliham
Publishing Director Katie Cowan

Photographer Louise Lister
Stylist Emma Knowles
Photochefs Peta Dent, Amal Webster

First published in Great Britain in 2021
by Dorling Kindersley Limited
DK, One Embassy Gardens, 8 Viaduct Gardens, London, SW11 7BW

The authorised representative in the EEA is Dorling Kindersley
Verlag GmbH. Arnulfstr. 124, 80636 Munich, Germany

Copyright © 2021 Dorling Kindersley Limited
A Penguin Random House Company
10 9 8 7 6 5 4 3 2 1
001–324523–May/2021

A CIP catalogue record for this book is available from the British Library.
ISBN: 978-0-2415-1015-5

Printed and bound in China

For the curious
www.dk.com

This book was made with Forest Stewardship Council ™ certified paper –
one small step in DK's commitment to a sustainable future.
For more information go to **www.dk.com/our-green-pledge**

Contents

Mediterranean Life

The Mediterranean diet is an approach to healthy eating that embraces variety, flavour, and nutrient-rich foods. Often referred to as the world's healthiest diet, it is backed by an abundance of scientific evidence showing that people who eat the Mediterranean way live longer and healthier lives.

Why eat the Mediterranean way?

It's no secret that people who eat a Mediterranean diet share many commonalities including a longer life expectancy, healthier hearts, and lower rates of chronic disease. The positive effects of the diet are far reaching and include lower levels of "bad" LDL cholesterol, better blood glucose (sugar) control, improved weight management, reduced risk of depression, as well as a lower incidence of some cancers, and Parkinson's and Alzheimer's diseases.

The Mediterranean diet is centred on minimally processed foods such as wholegrains, fruits, and vegetables, as well as seafood and fish, yogurt, pulses, seeds, and nuts. Also included are many foods often seen as an indulgence such as red wine, extra virgin olive oil, butter, and bread as, ultimately, balance and enjoyment are the core of this lifestyle.

Healthy fats

When it comes to good nutrition, not all fats are created equal but cutting out fat isn't encouraged on a Mediterranean diet. In fact, including healthy fats as part of a balanced diet can actually promote better health and may be the reason why people who follow a Mediterranean diet have healthier hearts than those who eat a traditional Western diet.

Healthy fats, including extra virgin olive oil, nuts and seeds, oily fish, and dairy foods like yogurt, are all included on the Mediterranean menu. Extra virgin olive oil features as the primary source of fat – it is an excellent source of monounsaturated fat and linoleic acid, both of which are good news for your heart. In particular, "extra virgin" and "virgin" oil are the least processed options while also containing the highest levels of beneficial polyphenols – the protective compound found in plants.

With the Mediterranean diet you simply swap sources of saturated and trans fats for foods with more monounsaturated and polyunsaturated fats. Choose foods like avocado, nuts, seeds, oily fish, extra virgin olive oil, and dairy products rather than filling up on too much red meat or deep-fried and processed options.

Fruits of the ocean

Seafood and fish are at the heart of this diet, offering a healthier and more sustainable alternative to red meat. Oily fish, such as sardines, herring, tuna, salmon, and mackerel, are all good sources of heart-healthy omega-3 fatty acids, a polyunsaturated fat that can help boost brain function including memory, concentration, and mood. Aim to eat fish or seafood at least twice a week and stick to smaller portions of red meat no more than two or three times a week. Along with seafood, plant-based sources of protein such as pulses, nuts, and seeds also feature heavily in the Mediterranean kitchen, making sure that the body receives the key nutrition it needs.

Fibre-rich foods

The Mediterranean diet also includes plenty of unrefined wholegrains and other fibre-rich foods such as vegetables and fruit to fuel your body with naturally slow-burning energy sources. A diet high in fibre is linked to better weight management and digestion, more stable moods, improved cholesterol levels, and reduced risk of some diseases including bowel cancer. Choose wholegrains such as oats, brown and black rice, quinoa, freekeh, and barley over the more refined and processed options. Adding legumes or pulses into your diet is also a great way to up your fibre intake and stay fuller for longer.

Many Mediterranean dishes are naturally bright and colourful, thanks to the fresh, seasonal produce that is key to creating such delicious, balanced meals. Fruit and vegetables are naturally full of antioxidants and polyphenols, which help combat signs of ageing and reduce the risk of inflammatory diseases. Eat five to ten portions of vegetables and fruit a day to get plenty of health-boosting antioxidants, polyphenols, vitamins, minerals, and fibre into your diet.

The Mediterranean lifestyle

It's not just the type of foods consumed in the Mediterranean diet that makes it so good for you, it is the way in which the food is cooked and eaten, with importance placed on fresh, quality produce, mealtimes, and balanced portion sizes.

Most Mediterranean dishes are designed to be enjoyed with family and friends, and this communal approach to eating helps to develop a sense of community and connection that is essential to wellbeing and happiness. Sharing dishes around the table also helps foster a healthy relationship with food, where the focus is on enjoyment and satiation, rather than restriction or control. Eating at the table is just one simple step that can promote mindfulness at mealtimes.

Another benefit of eating family-style share plates is that it encourages variety, which is the core of the Mediterranean diet. Including a wide range of ingredients in an array of colours is a simple way to help your body get a healthy of mix everything it needs to work at its best – choose mostly plant foods and try new ingredients, particularly as the seasons change. As you fill up on more nutrient-rich foods, you will help your body to thrive.

SHARED PLATES

From starters to tapas and light bites, these
dishes will add vibrancy to your table.
Perfect for sharing, they'll bring a sense of
communal enjoyment to group gatherings.

Spring greens and feta bruschetta

VEGETARIAN | PREP + COOK TIME **40 MINUTES** | SERVES **4**

Pesto alla genovese is a sauce originating in Genoa, Italy. It is traditionally made by pounding or grinding garlic cloves, pine nuts, basil, cheese, and olive oil together using a mortar and pestle. Today there are many variations of pesto, from this one with rocket and almonds, to others that use different fresh green herbs or even spinach or kale.

1 cup (150g) frozen broad beans, thawed (see tips)

170g asparagus, trimmed, sliced diagonally

$1/2$ cup (60g) frozen peas

8 slices sourdough bread (280g)

1 tbsp extra virgin olive oil

1 garlic clove, crushed

1 tbsp lemon juice

salt and freshly ground black pepper

90g drained marinated feta, crumbled

2 tbsp small fresh mint leaves

1 tsp finely grated lemon rind

rocket and almond pesto

60g rocket

1 cup (20g) fresh basil leaves

$1/2$ cup (70g) slivered almonds, roasted

1 garlic clove, crushed

1 tsp finely grated lemon rind

$1/3$ cup (25g) finely grated parmesan

$1/2$ cup (125ml) extra virgin olive oil

1 Cook the broad beans and asparagus in a medium saucepan of boiling water for 2 minutes. Add the peas, cook for 2 minutes; drain. Refresh in a bowl of iced water; drain. Remove grey skins from the broad beans.

2 To make the rocket and almond pesto, process the rocket, basil, almonds, garlic, lemon rind, parmesan, and 1 tablespoon of the olive oil until coarsely chopped. With the motor operating, add the remaining oil in a thin, steady stream until the mixture is smooth; season with salt and pepper to taste.

3 Cook the bread on a heated oiled grill plate (or pan or barbecue) for 1 minute on each side or until lightly charred. Spread $1/3$ cup (85g) pesto on the bread slices.

4 Heat the olive oil in a medium frying pan over a medium-high heat. Cook the garlic for 1 minute. Add the asparagus, beans, and peas; cook for 1 minute or until hot. Stir in the lemon juice; season with salt and pepper to taste.

5 Spoon the vegetable mixture onto the toasted bread; top with the feta, mint, and lemon rind.

TIPS

- If fresh broad beans are in season, you could use 575g fresh broad beans in the pod instead of frozen.
- Serving-sized portions of pesto can be frozen in small tightly-sealed containers for up to 3 months.

Roasted mushrooms with spinach, tomato, and ricotta

VEGETARIAN | PREP + COOK TIME **40 MINUTES** | SERVES **2**

Ricotta is a soft, sweet, moist cheese made from cow's milk, with a low fat content and a slightly grainy texture. The name roughly translates as "cooked again" and refers to ricotta's manufacture from a whey that is itself a by-product of other cheese making. Ricotta has been made on the Italian peninsula for centuries and has a special place in Italian cuisine.

4 large flat mushrooms (400g), trimmed

275g vine-ripened tomatoes

2 tbsp extra virgin olive oil

salt and freshly ground black pepper

2 garlic cloves, crushed

1 tbsp balsamic vinegar

12 sprigs fresh thyme

50g baby spinach leaves

1/4 cup (25g) fresh ricotta, crumbled

sourdough bread slices, toasted, to serve

1 Preheat oven 200°C (180°C fan/400°F/Gas 6). Line a large roasting pan with baking paper.

2 Place the mushrooms and tomatoes in the lined pan; drizzle evenly with half the olive oil. Season with salt and pepper.

3 Combine the garlic, vinegar, and remaining oil in a small bowl; drizzle over the mushrooms, then sprinkle with the thyme. Cover the pan loosely with baking paper; bake for 20 minutes.

4 Discard the top baking paper. Tuck the spinach leaves under the mushrooms and tomatoes. Top the mushrooms with the ricotta. Bake for 5 minutes or until vegetables are tender. Serve with toasted sourdough.

TIP

If vine-ripened tomatoes are not available, use cherry or roma (plum) tomatoes instead.

Cavolo nero fritters with pickled beetroot

VEGETARIAN | PREP + COOK TIME **35 MINUTES + STANDING** | SERVES **4**

Meaning "black cabbage" in Italian, cavolo nero is championed in many Italian dishes, especially those from the region of Tuscany. The traditional ingredient of minestrone and ribollita, cavolo nero is more delicate and sweet than its relative curly kale, while possessing many of the same nutritional benefits; it is rich in protein, fibre, antioxidants, and vitamins.

3 large courgettes (450g), coarsely grated

1 tsp fine sea salt

3 cavolo nero leaves (30g), trimmed, finely shredded

2 tbsp chopped fresh mint leaves

1/4 cup (40g) wholemeal plain flour

2 garlic cloves, crushed

2 eggs, lightly beaten

salt and freshly ground black pepper

1/3 cup (80ml) extra virgin olive oil

1 tbsp apple cider vinegar

1/2 tsp honey

100g Greek feta, crumbled

2 tbsp sunflower seeds, toasted

fresh mint leaves, to serve

pickled beetroot

3 small beetroot (300g), peeled, thinly sliced (see tips)

2 tbsp apple cider vinegar

1 Combine the courgette and salt in a colander; stand it in the sink for 10 minutes to drain. Using your hands, squeeze excess liquid from the courgette. Place the courgette, cavolo nero, mint, flour, garlic, and egg in a medium bowl; season with salt and pepper. Mix well to combine.

2 Meanwhile, make the pickled beetroot. Combine the beetroot and vinegar in a bowl; season with salt and pepper. Stand for 5 minutes. Drain; reserve the pickling liquid for the honey dressing. Set aside.

3 Heat half the olive oil in a large non-stick frying pan over a medium heat. Add an eighth of the courgette and kale mixture to the pan, flatten slightly; cook for 5 minutes on each side or until golden and crisp. Drain on paper towel; cover to keep warm. Repeat with the remaining mixture to make eight fritters.

4 Whisk the remaining oil, vinegar, honey, and reserved pickling liquid in a small bowl until combined.

5 Place the fritters on a platter, top with the beetroot and feta. Before serving, drizzle with the honey dressing and sprinkle with the sunflower seeds and mint leaves.

TIPS

▪ You can use a mandoline or V-slicer to slice the beetroot very thinly.

▪ Cooked fritters can be frozen; reheat for a quick breakfast option.

Sardine and golden tomato toasts

PESCATARIAN | PREP + COOK TIME **30 MINUTES + REFRIGERATION** | SERVES **4**

Sardines have long been relegated to "poor man's food", but this little fish is a powerhouse of nutrition: a serving of sardines can provide about 150 per cent of the recommended daily dose of vitamin B12, 13 per cent of vitamin B2, and one-quarter of niacin. It's also a source of omega-3, which has an array of health benefits related to its anti-inflammatory properties.

1 tsp fennel seeds, lightly crushed

2 tsp sea salt flakes

2 garlic cloves, finely chopped

salt and freshly ground black pepper

500g fresh sardines, cleaned, filleted, with tails intact (see tip)

1kg yellow cherry tomatoes

1/4 cup (60ml) extra virgin olive oil

1 loaf ciabatta bread (450g), sliced, toasted

small fresh basil leaves, to serve

lemon wedges, to serve

basil and caperberry oil

1 cup (20g) fresh basil leaves

1/2 cup (125ml) extra virgin olive oil

1/4 cup (40g) caperberries

2 tsp finely grated lemon rind

2 tbsp lemon juice

1 To make the basil and caperberry oil, blend or process the ingredients until smooth; season with salt and pepper to taste.

2 Combine the fennel seeds, salt, and garlic in a small bowl; season with salt and pepper. Rub the fennel mixture over the sardine fillets. Cover; refrigerate for 30 minutes.

3 Preheat the grill. Toss the tomatoes in half the olive oil on an oven tray. Place under the grill for 10 minutes or until the tomatoes are just starting to blister. Cool slightly.

4 Place the tomatoes along with the basil and caperberry oil in a large bowl; toss gently to combine. Season with salt and pepper to taste.

5 Heat the remaining oil in a large frying pan or grill plate; cook the sardines, in batches, for 2 minutes on each side or until cooked.

6 Place the sardines on toasted bread; spoon the tomato mixture on top, pressing gently to allow tomato juices to soak into the bread. Top with the basil leaves; serve with lemon wedges.

TIP

You can ask the fishmonger to clean and fillet the sardines for you.

Cauliflower pastilla triangles

VEGAN | PREP + COOK TIME **1 HOUR 20 MINUTES + STANDING** | MAKES **9**

Pastilla is a traditional Moroccan pie served on special occasions. Usually filled with a lightly spiced mix of poultry and nuts, this vegan version instead stars cauliflower. Saffron is one of the most expensive spices in the world by weight – it consists of the dried stigmas of the crocus plant and a kilogram of saffron requires 110,000–170,000 flowers.

pinch of saffron threads

1 tbsp hot water

2 tbsp extra virgin olive oil

2 medium red onions (340g), finely chopped

2 garlic cloves, crushed

1 tsp ground turmeric

1 tsp ground ginger

$^3/_4$ tsp ground cinnamon

$^1/_2$ small cauliflower (500g), finely chopped

salt

1 cup (160g) roasted blanched almonds, coarsely chopped

1 cup (30g) coarsely chopped fresh coriander leaves

1 cup (20g) coarsely chopped fresh flat-leaf parsley leaves

9 sheets filo pastry

$^1/_2$ cup (125ml) extra virgin olive oil, extra

lemon wedges, to serve

Greek yogurt, to serve (optional)

1 Combine the saffron and water in a small bowl.

2 Heat the olive oil in a large frying pan over a medium heat; cook the onion, garlic, turmeric, ginger, and $^1/_2$ teaspoon of the ground cinnamon for 5 minutes or until the onion softens. Add the cauliflower; cook, stirring, for 10 minutes or until tender. Season with salt. Add the saffron mixture; cook for 1 minute or until the water evaporates. Transfer to a large bowl; stir in the almonds and herbs. Leave to cool completely.

3 Preheat oven to 180°C (160°C fan/350°F/Gas 4). Oil an oven tray.

4 Brush one sheet of pastry with a little of the extra oil; cut in half lengthways, place one strip on top of the other. Keep the remaining sheets covered with baking paper topped with a clean, damp tea towel to prevent them from drying out.

5 Place $^1/_3$ cup cauliflower mixture in a corner of the pastry strip, leaving a 1cm border. Fold the opposite corner of the pastry diagonally across the filling to form a triangle; continue folding to the end of the pastry sheet, retaining the triangular shape. Place the triangle, seam-side down, on the oven tray. Repeat with the remaining pastry, olive oil, and cauliflower filling.

6 Brush the triangles with a little more oil; dust with the remaining cinnamon. Bake for 30 minutes or until the pastry is lightly browned.

7 Serve warm with lemon wedges and Greek yogurt, if you like.

Small bites

Tapas – small plates or appetizers – originate from Spain, but every Mediterranean country has their own version. Great for serving at parties, these bites can be enjoyed as a snack or starter, or combined to create a full sharing meal.

Dukkah prawn skewers

PESCATARIAN | PREP TIME **15 MINUTES** | SERVES **4**

Shell and devein 1.2kg uncooked large prawns, leaving the tails intact. Combine ¼ cup (40g) pistachio dukkah, 2 tablespoons of extra virgin olive oil, 2 crushed garlic cloves and 2 teaspoons of finely grated lemon rind in a large bowl; add the prawns, toss to coat in mixture. Thread prawns onto 8 bamboo or metal skewers. Heat a heavy-based frying pan over a high heat; cook the skewers, turning, until prawns change colour. Serve with lemon wedges.

Baked feta with roasted garlic, chilli, and olives

VEGETARIAN | PREP TIME **1 HOUR 25 MINUTES** | SERVES **10**

Preheat oven to 180°C (160°C fan/350°F/Gas 4). Place 10 peeled cloves of garlic and ¼ cup (60ml) extra virgin olive oil in a small ovenproof dish (ensure garlic is completely covered by oil). Cover with foil; bake for 30 minutes or until tender. Cool slightly. Increase oven to 200°C (180°C fan/400°F/Gas 6). Pat 700g Greek feta dry with paper towel. Cut into 4cm thick slices; place in an ovenproof dish, just large enough for feta to fit in a single layer. Pour ¼ cup (60ml) additional extra virgin olive oil and the garlic in oil over the feta; top with 2 sprigs fresh rosemary, 3 teaspoons of fresh oregano leaves, ⅓ cup (40g) small black olives and ½ thinly sliced fresh long red chilli. Bake for 40 minutes or until the feta is soft and lightly browned. Serve with toasted or grilled pita bread.

Stuffed courgette flowers

VEGETARIAN | PREP TIME **2 HOURS 30 MINUTES** | MAKES **18**

Combine 250g firm ricotta, 50g finely chopped Greek feta, 2 tablespoons of finely chopped fresh mint leaves, 2 teaspoons of finely grated lemon rind, ½ teaspoon of dried chilli flakes, 1 crushed garlic clove, and 1 egg yolk in a medium bowl; season with salt and pepper to taste. Carefully open 18 courgette flowers then remove the yellow stamens from inside the flowers. Spoon the ricotta mixture into the flowers, leaving a 1cm gap at the top. Twist petal tops to enclose the filling. Heat 2 tablespoons of extra virgin olive oil in a non-stick frying pan over a high heat; cook the flowers for 1 minute on each side or until light golden and heated through; season with salt and pepper to taste. Sprinkle with finely grated lemon rind and mint leaves.

CLOCKWISE from top

Grilled sardines with pangrattato

PESCATARIAN | PREP + COOK TIME **20 MINUTES** | SERVES **4**

Pangrattato is Italian for breadcrumbs. In southern parts of the country this crunchy bread topping was used as a substitute for the more expensive cheese. Recently it has become popular on its own merit as a delicious topping for vegetables, salads, and pasta, and is great sprinkled on crispy fried eggs. It is a perfect way to use up old, stale bread and save it from the bin.

750g fresh sardines, cleaned (see tips)

1/4 cup (60ml) extra virgin olive oil, plus extra to serve

salt and freshly ground black pepper

1 medium lemon (140g)

50g rocket leaves

1/3 cup watercress sprigs (see tips)

1/4 cup (40g) pine nuts, toasted (see tips)

pangrattato

2 tbsp extra virgin olive oil

1 cup (60g) coarsely chopped day-old bread

1 garlic clove, crushed

1/2 cup (10g) coarsely chopped fresh flat-leaf parsley

1/4 cup (40g) finely grated parmesan

1 To make pangrattato, heat the olive oil in a large frying pan over a medium heat; cook the bread, stirring, for 2 minutes or until golden. Add the garlic; cook, stirring, for 1 minute or until fragrant. Cool for 10 minutes. Place in a food processor with the parsley; pulse until coarse crumbs form. Stir in the parmesan; season with salt and pepper to taste.

2 Rub the sardines with 2 tablespoons of the olive oil; season with salt and pepper. Cook the sardines on a heated grill plate (or pan or barbecue) over a high heat for 2 minutes. Turn, cook for 1 minute or until cooked through.

3 Cut the lemon in half; juice one half, cut the remaining half into wedges. Place the rocket, watercress, pine nuts, lemon juice, and remaining oil in a medium bowl. Season with salt and pepper.

4 Place the rocket mixture on a platter; top with the sardines, then drizzle with a little more olive oil. Sprinkle with the pangrattato. Serve with the lemon wedges.

TIPS

- Ask the fishmonger to clean the sardines for you.
- Serve with any salad leaves instead of watercress, if you like.
- Substitute the pine nuts with your favourite toasted nuts or seeds.

Greek vegetable pie with yellow split pea dip

VEGETARIAN | PREP + COOK TIME **1 HOUR 15 MINUTES + STANDING & COOLING** | SERVES **8**

Although called a pie, this traditional Greek baked vegetable-and-herb-packed recipe is more like a frittata, as it contains no pastry. Kefalotyri is a semi-firm Greek sheep's or goat's milk cheese. Top sprinkled with fresh small mint leaves before serving, if you like.

250g courgettes, very thinly sliced

1 tsp fine sea salt

780g silverbeet (Swiss chard)

200g green beans, trimmed

125g Greek feta, crumbled

125g kefalotyri cheese or parmesan, coarsely grated

1/4 cup (10g) coarsely chopped fresh flat-leaf parsley leaves

2 tbsp chopped fresh dill

1 tbsp chopped fresh mint leaves

3/4 cup (50g) fresh breadcrumbs (see tips)

6 eggs, lightly beaten

1/4 cup (35g) sesame seeds, toasted

1 tbsp extra virgin olive oil

salt and freshly ground black pepper

8 small pita pockets, warmed

lemon wedges, to serve

yellow split pea dip

1 cup (200g) dried yellow split peas

1 small onion (80g), chopped

4 garlic cloves, bruised

1 tsp ground cumin

1 tsp ground coriander

1/3 cup (80ml) extra virgin olive oil

1/4 cup (60ml) lemon juice

TIP

The breadcrumbs are best made from bread that is about 3 days old.

1 Preheat oven to 180°C (160°C fan/350°F/Gas 4). Oil a 24cm springform pan; line the bottom with baking paper.

2 Combine the courgettes and salt in a colander over a bowl; stand for 30 minutes. Rinse the courgettes under cold water; drain. Trim stems from the silverbeet; discard stems. You will need 300g leaves.

3 Meanwhile, cook the beans in a large saucepan of boiling water for 5 minutes or until tender. Remove and finely chop the beans.

4 Add the silverbeet to the water in the pan, return to the boil; drain immediately. Refresh under cold running water; drain well. Squeeze the silverbeet to remove excess moisture; pat dry with paper towel. Finely chop the silverbeet.

5 Place the courgette, beans, and silverbeet in a large bowl with the cheeses, herbs, breadcrumbs, egg, sesame seeds, and olive oil; mix well to combine. Season with salt and pepper. Spoon the mixture into the lined pan; smooth the surface.

6 Bake the pie for 35 minutes or until golden and set. Leave in the pan for 15 minutes.

7 Meanwhile, to make the yellow split pea dip, place the split peas in a small saucepan with enough cold water to just cover; bring to the boil. Drain; rinse. Return the peas to the pan with the onion and garlic, add enough cold water to cover by 6cm; bring to the boil. Reduce heat to medium; cook for 25 minutes or until the peas are tender and beginning to collapse. Drain. Cool to room temperature.

8 Process the split pea mixture and spices until smooth. With the motor operating, gradually add the olive oil in a steady stream, then add the lemon juice in a steady stream. Season with salt and pepper to taste.

9 Serve pie warm or at room temperature with the dip, pitta bread, and lemon wedges.

Wholegrain pizza marinara

PESCATARIAN | PREP + COOK TIME **45 MINUTES + REFRIGERATION AND STANDING** | SERVES **4**

Pizza marinara is a style of Neapolitan pizza that is made with no cheese. This healthy substitute for a lazy Friday night takeaway pizza ditches the white base and greasy calorie-laden cheese for low-fat seafood chilli marinara with a crispy wholemeal crust. Ask your fishmonger to clean the octopus for you, if you prefer.

8 uncooked medium king prawns (180g)

4 cleaned baby octopus (360g), halved lengthways

2 fresh long red chillies, finely chopped

2 garlic cloves, crushed

2 tsp finely grated lemon rind

2 tbsp extra virgin olive oil

salt and freshly ground black pepper

200g cherry tomatoes, halved

50g rocket leaves

1 tbsp lemon juice

lemon wedges, to serve

dough

1/4 cup (45g) fine bulgur (bulgur wheat)

1/2 cup (125ml) warm water

1/2 tsp caster sugar

1 tsp dried yeast

2/3 cup (100g) plain flour

2/3 cup (100g) wholemeal plain flour

1 Peel and the devein prawns; place in a large bowl with the octopus. Combine the chilli, garlic, lemon rind, and olive oil in a bowl; season with salt and pepper to taste. Place half the chilli mixture in a small bowl, cover; refrigerate. Add the remaining chilli mixture to the prawns and octopus; toss to coat in the mixture. Cover; refrigerate for 1 hour.

2 Meanwhile, make the dough. Place the bulgur in a heatproof bowl; cover with boiling water; stand, covered, for 30 minutes. Rinse under cold water; drain. Combine the warm water, sugar, and yeast in a small jug, cover; stand in a warm place for 10 minutes or until frothy. Combine the bulgur and sifted flours in a medium bowl. Add the yeast mixture; mix to a soft dough. Knead the dough on a floured surface for 5 minutes or until smooth and elastic. Place the dough in an oiled medium bowl. Cover; stand in a warm place for 45 minutes or until doubled in size.

3 Preheat oven to 220°C (200°C fan/425°F/Gas 7). Lightly oil four large oven trays.

4 Divide the dough into four. Roll each piece into a 15cm round; place on the oven trays. Bake pizza bases, in batches, for 8 minutes or until partially cooked. Top with the seafood mixture and tomatoes. Bake pizzas, in batches, for a further 10 minutes or until the bases are crisp and the seafood is just cooked. Drizzle with the reserved chilli mixture.

5 Place the rocket and lemon juice in a small bowl; toss gently to coat. Season with salt and pepper to taste.

6 Top pizzas with the rocket mixture; serve with lemon wedges.

Lamb kofta, white bean, and beetroot tzatziki

PREP + COOK TIME **40 MINUTES** | SERVES **4**

Beetroot is a firm, round root vegetable, notable for its distinct red colour and earthy, sweet flavour. Beetroot is a good source of iron and folate. It also contains nitrates, betaine, magnesium, and other antioxidants. More recent health claims suggest beetroot can help lower blood pressure, boost exercise performance, and prevent dementia.

400g can butter beans, drained, rinsed

1 tbsp lemon juice

2 tbsp fresh oregano leaves

2 tbsp extra virgin olive oil

salt and freshly ground black pepper

1/2 cup (35g) fresh breadcrumbs

2 tbsp milk

600g minced lamb

1 tsp ground allspice

1/3 cup coarsely chopped fresh oregano, extra

100g Greek feta, crumbled

1 baby cos lettuce, trimmed, leaves separated

lemon slices, to serve (optional)

beetroot tzatziki

200g beetroot, peeled, coarsely grated

1 cup (280g) Greek yogurt

2 tbsp chopped fresh mint leaves

1 garlic clove, crushed

1 tbsp finely grated lemon rind

1 To make the beetroot tzatziki, combine the ingredients in a medium bowl; season with salt and pepper to taste.

2 Combine the butter beans, lemon juice, oregano leaves, and half the olive oil in a medium bowl; season with salt and pepper to taste.

3 Place the breadcrumbs and milk in a medium bowl; stand for 3 minutes or until the milk has been absorbed. Add the lamb, allspice, and extra oregano; season with salt and pepper. Using your hands, work the mixture until well combined. Add the feta; mix until combined. Roll heaped tablespoon measures of lamb mixture into ball shapes. Thread onto 8 skewers.

4 Heat the remaining oil in a large non-stick frying pan over a medium-high heat; cook the kofta, turning occasionally, for 10 minutes or until browned and cooked through.

5 Serve the kofta on the lettuce with the bean mixture, the beetroot tzatziki, and pan-fried lemon slices if using.

TIPS

- If you don't have metal skewers, thread kofta onto bamboo skewers that have been soaked in boiling water for 10 minutes to prevent them burning during cooking.
- Cooked or uncooked kofta can be frozen for up to 3 months; thaw in the fridge.

Spanish fish skewers with smoky romesco sauce

PESCATARIAN | PREP + COOK TIME **1 HOUR 45 MINUTES + COOLING AND REFRIGERATION** | SERVES **4**

Romesco is a traditional northern Spanish sauce, much like pesto in texture, made from a mixture of nuts and fire-roasted capsicum that often accompanies fish and seafood. Romesco also goes well with barbecued meats or char-grilled vegetables such as aubergine and courgette.

2 small red capsicums (peppers) (300g), quartered

3 garlic cloves, unpeeled

750g skinless boneless firm white fish fillets, cut into 2.5cm pieces

2 tsp smoked paprika

1/3 cup (80ml) extra virgin olive oil

2 tsp finely grated lemon rind

2 tbsp finely chopped fresh flat-leaf parsley leaves

salt and freshly ground black pepper

24 fresh bay leaves

1/4 cup (40g) blanched almonds

2 tbsp lemon juice

2 medium lemons (280g), halved

1   Preheat the grill on high heat. Place the capsicum, skin-side up, and garlic on an oven tray. Cook under the grill for 15 minutes or until the skins are blackened. Transfer to a medium bowl. Cover with plastic wrap (cling film); cool.

2   Combine the fish with half the paprika, half the olive oil, the lemon rind, and parsley in a medium bowl; season with salt and pepper. Thread the fish and bay leaves onto 12 skewers. Place on a tray; cover, refrigerate.

3   Meanwhile, remove and discard skins from the capsicum and garlic. Process the capsicum, garlic, almonds, lemon juice, remaining paprika, and remaining olive oil until almost smooth. Transfer the romesco to a small bowl; season with salt and pepper to taste.

4   Cook the fish skewers in a large heavy-based frying pan over a medium-high heat for 4 minutes or until browned all over and cooked through. Add lemon halves to pan; cook for 1 minute or until browned.

5   Serve the fish skewers with the romesco sauce and cooked lemon halves.

TIPS

- You will need 12 bamboo or metal skewers for this recipe. Soak the bamboo skewers for 10 minutes in boiling water before using to prevent them burning during cooking; oil metal skewers to prevent sticking.
- Romesco can be made a day ahead; keep covered in the fridge.

Pan con tomate

VEGETARIAN | PREP + COOK TIME **15 MINUTES** | SERVES **2**

Pan con tomate is a staple breakfast in Spain and is a humble dish full of robust flavours. The key to its simplicity is to have summer-ripe tomatoes, good-quality bread, and delicious olive oil. You could serve this as a starter at a party, or pair with a hearty salad for a light summer dinner. Serve topped with a fried or soft-boiled egg for a delicious twist.

500g cherry tomatoes on the vine

1/4 cup (60ml) extra virgin olive oil

salt and freshly ground black pepper

4 large slices sourdough bread (280g)

1 garlic clove, halved

70g goat's cheese, crumbled

2 tbsp fresh oregano leaves

1 Preheat oven to 200°C (180°C fan/400°F/Gas 6). Line an oven tray with baking paper.

2 Place the tomatoes on the tray, drizzle with 2 tablespoons of olive oil; season with salt and pepper. Roast for 10 minutes or until the skins burst and the tomatoes have softened.

3 Drizzle the bread with the remaining olive oil. Cook on a heated grill plate (or barbecue) for 1 minute each side or until lightly charred. Rub the grilled bread slices with the cut side of the garlic.

4 Squash the warm tomatoes onto the toasted bread slices. Top with the goat's cheese and oregano.

TIP

If cherry tomatoes on the vine are unavailable, use regular cherry or plum tomatoes instead.

FAMILY
TABLE

These delicious dishes are designed to be shared around a communal table with family and friends – a philosophy that lies at the heart of Mediterranean eating.

Cumin baked beans

VEGAN | PREP + COOK TIME **1 HOUR 20 MINUTES + OVERNIGHT SOAKING** | SERVES **6**

Beans are a great vegan option that are packed with protein and fibre. Dried beans give a better flavour and texture than canned, though canned beans will work fine in this recipe. Take leftover baked beans to work for a delicious lunch that has none of the added sugar or salt of the supermarket version.

400g dried white beans

2 tbsp extra virgin olive oil

2 medium onions (300g), finely chopped

8 garlic cloves, thinly sliced

1 tsp ground cumin

2 fresh long red chillies, thinly sliced

$\frac{1}{4}$ cup (70g) tomato paste

3 large tomatoes (660g), coarsely chopped

3 cups (750ml) vegetable stock

2 tbsp coarsely chopped fresh oregano

salt and freshly ground black pepper

grilled sourdough bread, to serve

fresh oregano leaves, to serve (optional)

1 Place the beans in a large bowl, cover with cold water; stand overnight. Drain. Rinse under cold water; drain.

2 Place the beans in a medium saucepan, cover with water; bring to the boil over a high heat. Boil for 30 minutes or until the beans are almost tender. Drain.

3 Heat the olive oil in a large heavy-based saucepan over a medium heat. Add the onion, garlic, cumin, and chilli; cook, stirring occasionally, for 7 minutes or until the onion is golden. Add the tomato paste, tomatoes, and stock; bring to the boil. Reduce heat to medium, cook, covered, for 10 minutes or until the sauce thickens slightly.

4 Add the beans to the pan; cook, covered, stirring occasionally, for 10 minutes. Remove lid; cook for 10 minutes or until the beans are tender. Stir in the chopped oregano; season with salt and pepper to taste.

5 Serve cumin baked beans with grilled bread, and fresh oregano if desired.

TIP

You will need to start this recipe the day before. Or to save time, use 3 x 400g cans cannellini beans, drained and rinsed, instead of soaking dried beans.

Green minestrone with pesto

VEGETARIAN | PREP + COOK TIME **35 MINUTES** | SERVES **4**

There is no set recipe for minestrone, which is traditionally made with whatever vegetables
are in season at the time of cooking. Commonly the soup contains borlotti beans, but
ours instead uses cannellini beans and substitutes tomato for freshly made pesto
and bright green vegetables.

2 tbsp extra virgin olive oil

1 tsp finely chopped fresh sage leaves

2 garlic cloves, finely chopped

1 medium leek (350g), finely chopped

1 medium parsnip (250g), cut into 1cm cubes

2 trimmed celery stalks (200g), thinly sliced

150g curly kale, stems discarded, torn into pieces

6 cups (1.5 litres) vegetable stock

150g green beans, trimmed, cut into 2cm lengths
on the diagonal

2 medium courgettes (240g), halved lengthways,
thinly sliced

400g can cannellini beans, drained, rinsed

salt and freshly ground black pepper

pesto

2 cups (40g) fresh basil leaves

$1/3$ cup (25g) finely grated parmesan

$1/4$ cup (40g) pine nuts, toasted

$1/2$ garlic clove, peeled

$1/2$ cup (125ml) extra virgin olive oil

1 Heat the olive oil in a large saucepan over a medium heat. Cook the sage,
garlic, and leek, stirring, for 3 minutes or until the leek is soft. Add the
parsnip, celery, and kale; cook, stirring, for 2 minutes or until the kale is
bright green. Add the stock, bring to the boil; reduce heat to low. Simmer
for 15 minutes or until the parsnip is almost tender.

2 Add the green beans, courgette, and cannellini beans; cook for 5 minutes
or until the courgette is just tender. Season with salt and pepper to taste.

3 Meanwhile, make the pesto. Blend or process the ingredients until
smooth. Transfer to a small bowl; season with salt and pepper to taste.

4 Ladle the soup into bowls. Serve topped with the pesto.

TIPS

- The soup can be made a day ahead; keep covered
  in the fridge.
- The pesto can be made 3 days ahead; keep tightly
  covered, in a small airtight container, in the fridge.

Spaghettini niçoise

PESCATARIAN | PREP + COOK TIME **30 MINUTES** | SERVES **4**

This riff on the classic French favourite, salad niçoise, is equally enjoyable served warm or at room temperature. Easy to prepare in advance, it's a great addition to your repertoire of workday lunches and makes excellent picnic fare. Omit the chilli if you prefer.

250g spaghettini

4 eggs

425g canned tuna chunks in olive oil, drained, flaked (see tip)

1/3 cup (55g) pitted Kalamata olives, coarsely chopped

250g cherry tomatoes, halved

1/3 cup (50g) pine nuts, toasted

100g rocket leaves

salt and freshly ground black pepper

1/2 tsp dried chilli flakes

lemon mustard dressing

2 tbsp extra virgin olive oil

1 tbsp finely grated lemon rind

1/4 cup (60ml) lemon juice

1 garlic clove, crushed

1 tbsp Dijon mustard

1 tbsp capers

1 Make the lemon mustard dressing. Place the ingredients in a screw-top jar; shake well. Season with salt and pepper to taste.

2 Cook the pasta in a large saucepan of boiling salted water until almost tender; drain. Return to pan.

3 Meanwhile, place the eggs in a small saucepan, cover with cold water; bring to the boil. Cook for 2 minutes or until soft-boiled; drain. Rinse under cold water; drain. When cool enough to handle, peel the eggs.

4 Add the tuna, olives, tomatoes, pine nuts, rocket, and dressing to the pasta in the pan; toss gently. Season with salt and pepper to taste.

5 Serve the pasta topped with halved soft-boiled eggs and chilli flakes.

TIP

You can grill tuna steaks for 1 minute each side on a heated oiled grill pan (or barbecue) instead of using canned tuna, if you like.

Prawn, pea, and broad bean frittata

PESCATARIAN | PREP + COOK TIME **1 HOUR** | SERVES **4**

Derived from the Italian word *friggere* which roughly translates as "fried", a frittata is an amazingly versatile dish – the perfect vehicle for using up leftovers, while relatively simple to cook. It also makes the best packed lunch for work or school, as it can be eaten heated or cool. Serve accompanied with a simple green salad for a complete meal.

$^1/_2$ cup (30g) fresh flat-leaf parsley leaves

$^1/_3$ cup (8g) fresh dill

6 eggs

$^1/_2$ cup (125ml) buttermilk

2 tbsp store-bought dry breadcrumbs

salt and freshly ground black pepper

$1^1/_2$ cups (225g) frozen broad beans

2 tbsp extra virgin olive oil

2 medium courgettes (240g), halved lengthways, thinly sliced

3 green onions (spring onions), thinly sliced

2 garlic cloves, crushed

2 cups (240g) frozen peas, thawed

500g cooked medium king prawns, shelled, deveined

$^1/_3$ cup (80g) firm ricotta

lemon halves, to serve

1 Coarsely chop half the herbs; reserve remaining herbs. Whisk the chopped herbs, eggs, buttermilk, and breadcrumbs in a large bowl; season with salt and pepper.

2 Cook the broad beans in a large saucepan of boiling water for 2 minutes or until just tender; drain. Refresh under cold running water, drain well. Remove grey skins.

3 Preheat oven to 180°C (160°C fan/350°F/Gas 4).

4 Heat the olive oil in a 21cm ovenproof frying pan over a medium heat; cook the courgette and green onion, stirring, for 5 minutes or until soft. Add the garlic, peas, and broad beans; cook, stirring, for 1 minute or until fragrant. Add the egg mixture, gently shake pan to distribute mixture; reduce heat to low-medium. Cook, without stirring, for 5 minutes or until the edge is set. Top with the prawns and crumbled ricotta.

5 Bake the frittata for 20 minutes or until the centre is just firm.

6 Serve the frittata with the remaining herbs and the lemon halves.

TIP

If you don't have an ovenproof frying pan, wrap the handle of your pan in several layers of foil.

Aubergine parmigiana

VEGETARIAN | PREP + COOK TIME **1 HOUR 15 MINUTES** | SERVES **4**

With its national colours of red, white, and green, this layered dish is pure Italian comfort food. Aubergine is sliced and shallow-fried until golden on both sides and soft on the inside. Bake until the aubergine becomes melt-in-your-mouth tender. Serve with a rocket salad and crusty bread or stir through cooked short pasta.

²/₃ cup (160ml) extra virgin olive oil

1 medium onion (150g), finely chopped

2 garlic cloves, crushed

400g can chopped tomatoes

2 cups (560g) bottled tomato passata

¹/₄ tsp dried chilli flakes

salt and freshly ground black pepper

2 medium aubergines (600g), thickly sliced

¹/₄ cup (35g) plain flour

¹/₃ cup (7g) fresh basil leaves

200g bocconcini, thinly sliced (see tip)

²/₃ cup (50g) finely grated parmesan

¹/₂ tsp sweet paprika

small basil leaves, extra, to serve

1   Preheat oven to 180°C (160°C fan/350°F/Gas 4).

2   Heat 1 tablespoon of oil in a large frying pan over a medium heat; cook onion, stirring, until soft. Add the garlic; cook, stirring, until fragrant. Stir in the tomatoes, passata, and chilli; season with salt and pepper to taste. Transfer mixture to a medium jug.

3   Toss the aubergine in flour to coat; shake off excess. Heat the remaining olive oil in the same cleaned pan; cook the aubergine in batches, until browned on both sides. Drain on paper towel.

4   Layer half the aubergine in a 26cm round, 5cm deep ovenproof dish; season with salt and pepper. Top with half the tomato mixture, the basil, and the bocconcini. Repeat layering, finishing with parmesan; sprinkle with paprika.

5   Bake, covered, for 30 minutes. Uncover, bake for a further 15 minutes or until browned and tender. Serve topped with the extra basil.

TIPS

Bocconcini are baby mozzarella cheese balls, also often called mozzarella pearls.

Roast tomato soup with broccoli pesto

PREP + COOK TIME **1 HOUR + STANDING** | SERVES **4**

Tomatoes feature heavily in Mediterranean dishes, both in their raw state and cooked. While they are both nutritious and extremely tasty picked straight from the vine, cooking tomatoes increases their levels of lycopene, a phytochemical with significant antioxidant properties that's responsible for the bright red colour of the vegetable.

1kg vine-ripened tomatoes, quartered

3 garlic cloves, unpeeled

3 sprigs fresh thyme

1 medium onion (150g), chopped

salt and freshly ground black pepper

1/3 cup (80ml) extra virgin olive oil

3 cups (750ml) chicken stock

1 tbsp pine nuts, toasted

small fresh basil leaves, to serve

broccoli pesto

100g broccoli, chopped

1 garlic clove, crushed

1 1/2 tbsp pine nuts, toasted

1 1/2 tbsp finely grated parmesan

1 1/2 tbsp coarsely chopped fresh basil leaves

1/4 cup (60ml) extra virgin olive oil

1 Preheat oven to 220°C (200°C fan/425°F/Gas 7).

2 Place the tomatoes, garlic, thyme, and onion in a roasting pan; season with salt and pepper. Drizzle with 1/4 cup (60ml) of the olive oil; toss to coat the tomatoes. Roast for 30 minutes or until the tomatoes are very soft and browned around the edges.

3 Meanwhile, make the broccoli pesto. Cook the broccoli in a small saucepan of boiling water for 2 minutes; drain. Refresh under cold running water; drain well. Process the broccoli, garlic, pine nuts, parmesan, and basil until finely chopped. With the motor operating, gradually pour in the olive oil; process until combined. Season with salt and pepper to taste.

4 Transfer the roasted tomatoes and onion to a medium saucepan. Remove the thyme stalks. Squeeze the garlic out of skins; add to the tomato mixture. Add the stock to the pan and bring to the boil. Cool for 10 minutes. Blend or process the mixture until smooth; return the soup to the pan. Stir over a low heat until hot; season with salt and pepper to taste.

5 Ladle the soup into bowls; top with the broccoli pesto, pine nuts, and basil. Drizzle with the remaining olive oil.

TIPS

- To make this recipe vegetarian, use vegetable stock instead of chicken stock and use a vegetarian parmesan in the pesto – make sure it doesn't contain animal rennet.
- The soup and broccoli pesto are suitable to freeze, separately, for up to 3 months.

Spinach and yogurt flatbreads with Greek bean salad

VEGETARIAN | PREP + COOK TIME **45 MINUTES + STANDING** | SERVES **4**

Most people in the Mediterranean region could not imagine a day going by without the consumption of bread in one form or another. Fresh bread is surely one of the world's greatest comforts, and these simple flatbreads are a hassle-free way of preparing your own. Perfect to accompany a light lunch or dinner, or to enjoy as a light meal on its own.

250g frozen chopped spinach, thawed

1 cup (150g) self-raising flour

$^1/_2$ cup (140g) Greek yogurt

1 garlic clove, crushed

salt and freshly ground black pepper

2 tbsp extra virgin olive oil

200g tzatziki

lemon wedges, to serve

Greek bean salad

125g mixed cherry tomatoes, halved

1 medium cucumber (130g), quartered lengthways, sliced

$^1/_2$ cup (100g) canned cannellini beans, drained, rinsed

$^1/_4$ cup (30g) pitted black olives, halved

$^1/_4$ cup (3g) loosely packed fresh oregano leaves

100g Greek feta, crumbled

1   Place the spinach in a clean tea towel. Squeeze over a sink to remove as much excess liquid as possible. Place the spinach, flour, yogurt, and garlic in a large bowl; season with salt and pepper. Use your hands to bring the ingredients together and form a rough dough. Cover; stand dough for 1 hour.

2   Make the Greek bean salad. Place the ingredients in a large bowl; toss gently to combine. Season with salt and pepper to taste.

3   Divide the dough into eight balls. Roll out each ball of dough on a floured surface until 2mm thick.

4   Heat 1 teaspoon of the olive oil in a large heavy-based frying pan over a medium heat; cook one flatbread for 1 minute on each side or until golden. Remove from pan; cover to keep warm (see tips). Repeat with the remaining oil and dough.

5   Top flatbreads evenly with tzatziki and salad; serve with lemon wedges.

TIPS

- Keep flatbread warm in a preheated 130°C (110°C fan/250°F/Gas $^1/_2$) oven.
- Make the spinach dough a day ahead, cover and refrigerate until needed. Bring to room temperature before rolling out.

Chicken, courgette, and freekeh soup

PREP + COOK TIME **45 MINUTES** | SERVES **4**

Freekeh is made from roasted young green wheat. Nutritionally freekeh stacks up impressively; it has a low GI, four times the fibre of brown rice, and is higher in protein than regular wheat. The name freekeh comes from the word *farik*, which refers to the way that freekeh is threshed, or "rubbed", to remove its tough and inedible outer bran layer.

½ cup (100g) cracked green-wheat freekeh (see tips)

1 tbsp extra virgin olive oil

1 medium leek (350g), white part only, halved, thinly sliced

4 garlic cloves, thinly sliced

5 cups (1.25 litres) water (see tips)

4 chicken thigh fillets (680g)

150g green beans, trimmed, cut into 2cm lengths

salt and freshly ground black pepper

1 large courgette (150g), halved lengthways, thinly sliced

½ cup (60g) frozen peas

1 tsp finely grated lemon rind

2 tbsp lemon juice

2 tbsp chopped fresh flat-leaf parsley leaves

1 Place the freekeh in a medium saucepan, cover with water; bring to the boil. Reduce heat to low; cook, partially covered, for 15 minutes or until almost tender. Drain.

2 Meanwhile, heat the olive oil in a large saucepan over a medium heat; cook the leek, stirring, for 4 minutes or until softened. Add the garlic; cook, stirring, for 2 minutes.

3 Add the water and chicken, bring to the boil; reduce heat to low. Cook, covered, for 12 minutes or until the chicken is cooked. Remove the chicken from the stock; shred the meat. Return the shredded chicken to the pan with the green beans and freekeh, season with salt and pepper to taste; cook for 5 minutes. Add the courgette and peas; cook for 3 minutes or until tender. Stir in the lemon rind and juice.

4 Ladle the soup into bowls; top with parsley. Season with salt and pepper to taste.

TIPS

- Freekeh is a wheat product so it does contain gluten; it is available from health food stores and some supermarkets.
- For a more intense flavour, use homemade chicken stock instead of water.

Mushrooms

Mushrooms are a great source of fibre, protein, vitamin C, B vitamins, calcium, minerals, and selenium. Studies have shown they can help to reduce blood pressure and cholesterol, enhance the immune system, and assist in fighting many types of cancer.

Mushroom with almond picada

VEGAN | PREP + COOK TIME **45 MINUTES** | SERVES **2**

Preheat the oven to 200°C (180°C fan/400°F/Gas 6). Process 1 slice of day-old bread, 1 chopped garlic clove, $1/4$ cup (40g) natural almonds and $1/2$ cup (30g) fresh flat-leaf parsley until coarsely chopped. Scatter the mixture over 6 medium (600g) portobello mushrooms and 250g grape (cherry) tomatoes on a baking-paper-lined oven tray. Drizzle with $1/4$ cup (60ml) olive oil. Cover with foil. Bake for 15 minutes. Remove foil; bake for a further 15 minutes or until tender. Serve sprinkled with lemon rind strips and chopped fresh chilli.

Mushroom toastie

VEGETARIAN | PREP TIME **20 MINUTES** | MAKES **4**

Peel 4 portobello mushrooms (400g), trim stalks level with the cap. Brush one side of 4 thick slices of sourdough bread with a little olive oil. Place slices, oiled-side down, on a hot sandwich press, close; cook until lightly toasted. Brush each mushroom with 2 tablespoons of pesto; place the mushrooms on bread in the press, cover with baking paper. Close press; cook for 5 minutes or until the mushrooms are tender and the bread is golden. Top mushrooms with 100g crumbled feta; drizzle with a little olive oil. Serve with lemon wedges.

Mushroom and dill pilaf

VEGAN | PREP + COOK TIME **20 MINUTES** | SERVES **2**

Heat 2 tablespoons of olive oil in a frying pan over a high heat; cook 250g swiss brown (brown) mushrooms for 8 minutes or until browned and tender. Remove from the pan. To the pan, add 250g packet microwave brown basmati rice, 2 finely chopped green onions (spring onions), 1 teaspoon smoked paprika, and 2 tablespoons each of pistachios and currants; cook, stirring, for 5 minutes or until heated through. Stir in $1/2$ cup (14g) coarsely chopped dill and the mushrooms.

Mushroom and radicchio salad

VEGETARIAN | PREP TIME **15 MINUTES** | SERVES **4**

Heat 2 tablespoons of olive oil in a large frying pan over a high heat; cook 300g oyster mushrooms and 2 teaspoons of thyme leaves, stirring occasionally, for 5 minutes or until browned. Remove from the pan; cool. In a large bowl, whisk $1^1/2$ tablespoons each of balsamic vinegar and extra virgin olive oil. Add $1/2$ head torn radicchio leaves, the mushrooms, and 2 tablespoons each of pepitas (pumpkin seeds) and shaved parmesan; toss gently to combine.

CLOCKWISE from top left

Chicken with courgette "noodles", feta, and salsa verde

PREP + COOK TIME **35 MINUTES** | SERVES **4**

While to a true Italian, these courgette "noodles" may seem like heresy, they are a great alternative to pasta when you are looking to have a light summer meal. They also help to increase your vegetable consumption and lower your overall calorie intake.

4 chicken breast fillets (800g), halved horizontally

1 tbsp extra virgin olive oil

5 medium courgette (500g)

$^1/_3$ cup (25g) flaked almonds, toasted

100g goat's feta, crumbled

$^1/_4$ cup (15g) fresh flat-leaf parsley leaves

salsa verde

$^1/_2$ cup (10g) coarsely chopped fresh flat-leaf parsley

$^1/_4$ cup (6g) coarsely chopped fresh basil

1 garlic clove, crushed

2 tsp capers

1 tsp Dijon mustard

$^1/_4$ cup (60ml) extra virgin olive oil

2 tsp red wine vinegar

salt and freshly ground black pepper

1 Season the chicken. Heat the olive oil in a large frying pan over a medium-high heat; cook the chicken, in batches, for 4 minutes on each side or until browned and cooked through. Transfer to a plate; stand, covered loosely with foil.

2 Meanwhile, using a vegetable spiralizer (see tip), cut the courgette into noodles.

3 Make the salsa verde. Combine the herbs, garlic, and capers in a small bowl; whisk in the mustard, olive oil, and vinegar until thickened. Season with salt and pepper to taste.

4 Top the courgette noodles with the chicken, spoonfuls of salsa verde, the almonds, feta, and parsley. Serve with the remaining salsa verde.

TIP

A spiralizer is a kitchen gadget that cuts vegetables into long thin spirals. If you don't have one, you can use a mandoline or V-slicer to create thin ribbons.

Grilled vegetable and capsicum relish paninis

VEGETARIAN | PREP + COOK TIME **50 MINUTES + COOLING** | SERVES **4**

These sandwiches definitely pack a punch in terms of flavours, with the smoky taste of the grill, the umami of the parmesan-rich pesto, and the bite of the capsicum relish. This relish can be made in advance and stored in an airtight container in the fridge for up to a week.

2 small aubergines (460g), cut into 1cm slices

200g patty pan squash, cut into 1cm slices

200g butternut pumpkin (butternut squash), peeled, thinly sliced

olive oil cooking spray

salt and freshly ground black pepper

4 mini baguette rolls (680g), halved lengthways

$1/3$ cup (65g) pesto

$1/3$ cup (80g) soft ricotta

$1/2$ cup rocket leaves

capsicum relish

1 tbsp extra virgin olive oil

1 small onion (80g), finely chopped

1 garlic clove, crushed

1 tsp ground cumin

$1/2$ tsp chilli powder

2 medium red capsicums (peppers) (400g), coarsely chopped

2 medium yellow capsicums (peppers) (400g), coarsely chopped

2 tbsp brown sugar

2 tbsp red wine vinegar

1 To make the capsicum relish, heat the olive oil in a medium frying pan over a medium heat. Add the onion, garlic, and spices; cook, covered, for 5 minutes. Add the capsicum; cook, covered, stirring occasionally, for 20 minutes or until soft. Stir in sugar and vinegar; cook until syrupy. Cool.

2 Meanwhile, spray the aubergine, squash, and pumpkin with oil; season with salt and pepper. Cook the vegetables, in batches, on a heated oiled grill plate (or pan or barbecue) over a medium-high heat for 3 minutes each side or until browned and tender.

3 Spread each roll with 1 tablespoon of the pesto and 1 tablespoon of ricotta; top evenly with the vegetables, relish, and rocket.

Roasted sumac chicken with baby vegetables

PREP + COOK TIME **1 HOUR 15 MINUTES** | SERVES **4**

This roast chicken makes the perfect family dinner, with any leftovers great for salads and sandwiches the next day. Sumac is a purple-red, astringent spice ground from berries growing on shrubs that flourish wild around the Mediterranean; it adds a tart, lemony flavour to dips and dressings, and goes well with barbecued meats.

30g butter, softened

1 tbsp sumac

1.4kg chicken

salt and freshly ground black pepper

500g baby beetroot, trimmed

250g baby carrots, trimmed

250g yellow baby carrots, trimmed

1 tbsp extra virgin olive oil

$\frac{1}{2}$ cup (25g) fresh mint leaves

100g Greek feta, crumbled (see tip)

2 tbsp store-bought pistachio dukkah

1 Preheat oven to 180°C/350°F.

2 Combine the butter and sumac in a small bowl. Rub the sumac butter all over the outside of the chicken; season with salt and pepper. Tie chicken legs together with kitchen string; place in a large roasting pan. Wrap the beetroot individually in foil; add to the pan with the chicken. Roast for 30 minutes.

3 Baste chicken with the pan juices. Toss the carrots in olive oil; season with salt and pepper and add to the pan. Roast for a further 35 minutes or until the chicken is cooked through and skin is golden brown. Cover the chicken loosely with foil; stand for 10 minutes.

4 Meanwhile, peel the beetroot and cut in half. Return beetroot to the pan.

5 Serve the roast chicken and vegetables with the mint, feta, and dukkah.

TIP

You can use goat's, sheep's, or cow's milk feta for this recipe.

58

Pea and barley risotto with garlic prawns

PREP + COOK TIME **1 HOUR** | SERVES **4**

Risotto is traditionally made using short-grain rice such as carnaroli or arborio, but here we use barley, a nutritious cereal grain that is higher in fibre than processed white rice. Soluble fibre has been shown to lower levels of blood cholesterol, while also improving the regulation of blood sugar. However, unlike rice, barley is not gluten-free.

¹/₄ cup (60ml) extra virgin olive oil

1 fresh long red chilli, finely chopped

4 garlic cloves, finely chopped

2 shallots (50g), finely chopped

1 cup (200g) pearl barley

4 cups (1 litre) chicken stock

1 cup (250ml) water

1 tbsp finely grated lemon rind

¹/₂ cup (60g) frozen peas

150g sugar snap peas, trimmed, halved lengthways

salt and freshly ground black pepper

400g uncooked peeled medium king prawns

extra finely grated lemon rind, to serve

1 Heat 1 tablespoon of olive oil in a large heavy-based saucepan over a low-medium heat, add the chilli, half the garlic, and the shallots; cook, stirring, for 3 minutes or until tender. Add the barley; cook, stirring, for 2 minutes or until lightly toasted. Add half the stock; bring to the boil. Reduce heat to low; cook, stirring occasionally, for 18 minutes or until the liquid has been absorbed. Add the remaining stock and the water; cook, stirring occasionally, for a further 18 minutes or until most of the liquid has been absorbed. Add the lemon rind, peas, and sugar snap peas; cook, stirring, for 3 minutes or until the vegetables are tender. Season with salt and pepper to taste.

2 Meanwhile, shell and devein the prawns, leaving the tails intact. Heat the remaining olive oil in a medium frying pan over a high heat; cook the prawns and the remaining garlic, stirring, for 5 minutes or until prawns are just cooked. Season with salt and pepper.

3 Divide the risotto among four bowls; top with the prawns and extra lemon rind.

Kale and spinach spanakopitas

VEGETARIAN | PREP + COOK TIME **1 HOUR 45 MINUTES** | MAKES **6**

Spanakopita is known the world over. A family favourite, this filo-crusted pie is eaten all across the regions of Greece. In rural areas the greens are often a mixture of spinach with leek, chard, or sorrel. Here we also add the superfood kale, a nutritious leafy cabbage, for an extra nutrient boost. Serve with Greek yogurt, if you like.

1.5kg silverbeet (Swiss chard)

350g green curly kale

400g Greek feta, crumbled

10 green onions (spring onions), finely chopped

$^1/_2$ cup (10g) finely chopped fresh dill

$^3/_4$ cup (18g) finely chopped fresh flat-leaf parsley

2 tsp finely grated lemon rind

$^1/_4$ cup (60ml) lemon juice

3 eggs, lightly beaten

freshly ground black pepper

80g butter, melted

750g fresh filo pastry

2 tsp sesame seeds

lemon wedges, to serve

1 Preheat oven to 180°C (160°C fan/350°F/Gas 4).

2 Trim 4cm off the stalks ends from the silverbeet and kale; discard. Rinse and drain the greens, leaving some water clinging. Tear kale leaves from the centre stem. Cut the white stalk from the silverbeet leaves, cutting into the leaf in a V-shape. Finely chop the stems and leaves from the greens, keeping them separate.

3 Heat a large heavy-based saucepan over a high heat; cook the stems, stirring occasionally, for 10 minutes or until softened. Drain well; transfer to a bowl. Add the chopped leaves to the pan; cook for 2 minutes or until wilted. Drain well; add to the bowl with the stems. When cool enough to handle, squeeze excess water from the greens mixture (this prevents the pies from becoming soggy).

4 Combine the greens, feta, green onion, herbs, lemon rind, lemon juice, and egg in a large bowl; season with freshly ground black pepper.

5 Butter six 2-cup (500ml), 18cm round, 3cm deep pie dishes. Butter half a sheet of pastry, fold in half to make a smaller rectangle; butter the top. Place in one of the dishes, allowing the pastry to overhang the edge. Keep the remaining sheets covered with baking paper topped with a clean, damp tea towel to prevent them from drying out. Repeat with two more sheets of pastry, stacking them in the dish. You will now have six layers. Place a sixth of the filling into the dish. Brush half a sheet of pastry with melted butter, fold in half crossways, brush with butter, fold in half again; trim to fit the top of the pie. Place over the filling, then fold in and scrunch the overhanging pastry. Brush the top of the pie with a little more melted butter. Sprinkle with sesame seeds. Repeat to make six pies in total.

6 Sprinkle a little water over each pie; this will prevent the pastry from burning. Bake for 35 minutes or until golden. Serve with lemon wedges.

TIP

You can make the spanakopitas up to the end of step 5, then put them into freezer bags and freeze for up to 1 month. Cook them from frozen, increasing the cooking time slightly until the pastry is golden and the filling is heated through.

Beef souvlaki with fennel and garlic yogurt

PREP + COOK TIME **40 MINUTES + REFRIGERATION** | SERVES **4**

There is something so comforting in these small pieces of meat cooked on skewers, with their smoky, grilled flavour and the pleasure of eating with your hands. You can use bamboo or metal skewers instead of rosemary skewers, if you like.

1 medium lemon (140g)

2 tbsp extra virgin olive oil

$1/3$ cup (80ml) dry white wine

1 tbsp finely chopped fresh rosemary

1 bay leaf, torn

2 garlic cloves, crushed

salt and freshly ground black pepper

1kg piece beef sirloin or rump, cut into 4cm pieces

8 fresh rosemary stalks

grilled Greek pita bread, to serve

fennel salad

2 medium fennel bulbs (600g)

2 tbsp extra virgin olive oil

1 tbsp red wine vinegar

$1/2$ cup (80g) mixed pitted olives

garlic yogurt

1 cup (280g) Greek yogurt

2 garlic cloves, crushed

1 Finely grate rind from the lemon. Remove the white pith; coarsely chop the flesh.

2 Combine the olive oil, lemon rind and flesh, wine, chopped rosemary, torn bay leaf, and garlic in a large non-reactive bowl; season with salt and pepper. Add the beef, toss to coat in the mixture. Cover; refrigerate for 1 hour or overnight.

3 To make the fennel salad, trim the base of the fennel bulbs; reserve the fronds. Using a mandoline or V-slicer, thinly slice the fennel lengthways; place in a bowl of iced water. Drain well, lightly pat dry. Place the fennel, half the reserved fennel fronds, olive oil, vinegar, and olives in a medium bowl; toss well to combine. Season with salt and pepper to taste.

4 To make the garlic yogurt, place the ingredients in a small bowl with the remaining fennel fronds; stir to combine. Season with salt and pepper to taste.

5 Bring the beef to room temperature. Evenly thread the beef onto the rosemary stalks.

6 Cook the skewers on a heated grill plate (or pan or barbecue) over a medium-high heat, turning occasionally, for 5 minutes for medium rare or until cooked as desired.

7 Serve skewers with the grilled pita, fennel salad, and garlic yogurt.

Paprika and cumin spiced roast chicken with chickpeas

PREP + COOK TIME **45 MINUTES** | SERVES **4**

Paprika is a ground spice made from dried sweet red capsicum, with grades including sweet, mild, smoked, and hot. The hotter types are usually combined with ground chilli peppers or cayenne pepper. Originating in central Mexico, paprika was brought to Spain in the 16th century, and is often used to add colour to many types of dishes as well as flavour.

4 garlic cloves, crushed

1 tbsp smoked paprika

1 tsp cumin seeds

$\frac{1}{2}$ cup (125ml) extra virgin olive oil

$\frac{1}{2}$ cup (140g) Greek yogurt

salt and freshly ground black pepper

4 x 200g chicken breast supremes (see tip)

400g can chickpeas, drained, rinsed

400g small cherry tomatoes

200g firm ricotta, broken into large chunks

$\frac{1}{4}$ cup (5g) coriander sprigs

$\frac{1}{4}$ cup (15g) fresh flat-leaf parsley leaves

1 Preheat oven to 240°C/475°F. Line a large roasting pan with baking paper.

2 Combine the garlic, paprika, cumin, and $\frac{1}{3}$ cup (80ml) of olive oil in a small bowl. Reserve 2 teaspoons of the spice oil mixture in another bowl and combine it with the yogurt; season with salt and pepper. Cover the yogurt mixture; refrigerate until required.

3 Rub 2 tablespoons of the remaining spice oil mixture over the chicken; season with salt and pepper. Heat the remaining olive oil in a large frying pan over a high heat; cook the chicken for 2 minutes each side or until browned. Transfer chicken to a lined pan. Roast the chicken for 10 minutes.

4 Reduce oven to 200°C (180°C fan/400°F/Gas 6). Combine the chickpeas, tomatoes, ricotta, and remaining spice oil mixture in a large bowl. Spoon the chickpea mixture around the chicken in the pan; season with salt and pepper. Roast for a further 15 minutes or until the chicken is cooked through.

5 Serve the chicken and chickpea mixture with the yogurt sauce, sprinkled with coriander and parsley.

TIP

Chicken supremes are chicken breasts with the skin on and wing bone still attached. They are available from some supermarkets or specialty poultry stores; you may need to order them in advance.

Za'atar fish with bulgur salad

PESCATARIAN | PREP + COOK TIME **30 MINUTES + STANDING** | SERVES **4**

Spices and herbs are integral to a Mediterranean diet, adding flavour to dishes without fat or sugar. Some of the most common spices found in Mediterranean cuisine include cumin, saffron, sumac, and za'atar. Common herbs of the region, used both in their fresh and dried forms, include oregano, sage, coriander, parsley, thyme, basil, and rosemary.

1 tbsp olive oil

1½ tbsp za'atar (see tips)

4 x 180g boneless white fish fillets (see tips)

salt and freshly ground black pepper

bulgur salad

1 medium red onion (170g), thinly sliced

1 cup (60g) fresh flat-leaf parsley

1 tbsp fresh thyme leaves

4 medium roma (plum) tomatoes (450g), coarsely chopped

100g radishes, thinly sliced

60g rocket leaves

¼ cup (40g) fine bulgur (bulgur wheat)

1 tsp ground sumac

2 tbsp lemon juice

¼ cup (60ml) extra virgin olive oil

1 Make the bulgur salad. Combine the ingredients in a large bowl; season with salt and pepper to taste. Stand for 15 minutes or until the bulgur is softened.

2 Combine the olive oil, za'atar, and fish in a large bowl; season with salt and pepper. Cook the fish in a heavy-based non-stick frying pan over a medium-high heat for 2 minutes on each side or until browned and cooked through.

3 Serve the fish with the bulgur salad.

TIPS

- Za'atar is a Middle Eastern spice mixture usually containing sesame seeds, dried oregano, or dried thyme, sumac, and sea salt. It is available in major supermarkets and Middle Eastern food stores.
- Salmon or trout can be used instead, if you like.

Pumpkin and goat's cheese lasagne

VEGETARIAN | PREP + COOK TIME **3 HOURS** | SERVES **10**

Though it's an Italian staple, lasagne originated in Ancient Greece – the word "lasagne" is derived from the Greek word *Laganon*, which is the first known form of pasta. The ingredients Italians use in their recipe will depend on the part of Italy their family came from, but this healthy, fresh veggie version provides a lighter take on the classic dish.

3.4kg butternut pumpkins (butternut squash), halved lengthways

2 tbsp extra virgin olive oil

salt and freshly ground black pepper

4 medium leeks (1.4kg), thinly sliced

4 garlic cloves, crushed

1/2 tsp ground nutmeg

1kg firm ricotta

3 egg yolks

1 tsp finely grated lemon rind

1 1/4 cups (100g) finely grated parmesan

1 cup (250ml) single cream

1/4 cup (3g) finely chopped fresh sage leaves

1 1/2 tbsp finely chopped fresh chives

6 1/2 fresh lasagne sheets

150g soft goat's cheese, crumbled

rocket and pepita salad

2 tsp lemon juice

1 tsp wholegrain mustard

1 1/2 tbsp extra virgin olive oil

100g rocket leaves

1/4 cup (50g) pepitas (pumpkin seeds), toasted

1 Preheat oven to 200°C (180°C fan/400°F/Gas 6).

2 Divide the pumpkin halves, skin-side up, between two large oven trays; drizzle each pumpkin half with 1 tablespoon of olive oil. Season with salt and pepper. Cover with foil; bake for 2 hours or until very tender. Cool. Remove the seeds, then peel away skin. Working in batches, place the pumpkin in a large sieve over a bowl; leave to drain excess liquid, reserve. Transfer pumpkin to a bowl; mash with a potato masher.

3 Heat the remaining olive oil in a large saucepan over a medium heat; cook the leek and garlic, stirring occasionally, for 10 minutes or until soft. Combine the leek mixture, mashed pumpkin, nutmeg, and reserved pumpkin liquid. Season with salt and pepper to taste.

4 Process the ricotta, egg yolks, and lemon rind, in batches until smooth. Add 1 cup (80g) of parmesan and the cream, pulse until just combined. Stir in the herbs. Season with salt and pepper.

5 Oil an ovenproof dish, around 24cm x 30cm x 6cm. Place 2 lasagne sheets in the bottom of the dish. Spoon over a third of the ricotta mixture; smooth the surface. Top with half the pumpkin mixture. Repeat layers, then top with 2 1/2 lasagne sheets and another third of ricotta mixture. Sprinkle with the goat's cheese and remaining parmesan. Cover with a layer of baking paper, then foil.

6 Bake lasagne for 50 minutes. Remove foil and paper; bake for a further 15 minutes or until golden and hot. Stand for 10 minutes.

7 Meanwhile, to make the rocket and pepita salad, combine the lemon juice, mustard, and olive oil in a large bowl; season with salt and pepper to taste. Add the rocket and pepitas; toss gently to combine.

8 Serve the lasagne with the salad.

Greek roast lamb leg with lemon potatoes and skordalia

PREP + COOK TIME **4 HOURS 45 MINUTES + REFRIGERATION** | SERVES **4**

Skordalia is a classic Greek accompaniment to meat – a kind of dip or spread – made from either potato or bread pureed with garlic, olive oil, lemon juice or vinegar, herbs and, occasionally, ground nuts. To serve, sprinkle the roast lamb with extra fresh lemon thyme sprigs, if you like.

2 garlic cloves, crushed

$1/2$ cup (125ml) lemon juice

2 tbsp extra virgin olive oil

1 tbsp fresh oregano leaves

1 tsp fresh lemon thyme leaves

2kg lamb leg

lemon wedges, to serve

skordalia

1 medium potato (200g), quartered

3 garlic cloves, quartered

1 tbsp lemon juice

1 tbsp white wine vinegar

2 tbsp water

$1/3$ cup (80ml) extra virgin olive oil

1 tbsp warm water

lemon potatoes

5 large potatoes, quartered

1 medium lemon (140g), rind peeled into 6 wide strips

2 tbsp lemon juice

2 tbsp extra virgin olive oil

salt and freshly ground black pepper

1 Combine the garlic, lemon juice, olive oil, oregano, and thyme leaves in a large non-reactive bowl; add the lamb, turn to coat in the mixture. Cover; refrigerate for 3 hours or overnight.

2 Preheat oven to 160°C (140°C fan/325°F/Gas 3).

3 Place the marinated lamb in a large roasting pan; roast for $3^{1}/2$ hours.

4 Meanwhile, to make the skordalia, boil, steam, or microwave the potato until tender; drain. Push the potato through a ricer or fine sieve into a medium bowl; cool for 10 minutes. Add the garlic, lemon juice, vinegar, and water to the potato; stir until well combined. Place the potato mixture in a blender; with the motor operating, gradually add the olive oil in a thin, steady stream, blending only until the skordalia thickens (do not over-mix or the sauce will become gluey). Stir in the warm water.

5 To make the lemon potatoes, combine the potato, lemon rind, lemon juice, and olive oil in a large bowl; season with salt and pepper. Place, in a single layer, on an oven tray.

6 Put the lemon potatoes in the oven; roast alongside the lamb for the last 30 minutes of lamb cooking time.

7 Remove the lamb from the oven; stand, covered loosely with foil.

8 Increase oven to 220°C/425°F; roast the potatoes a further 20 minutes or until golden.

9 Serve the roast lamb with the lemon potatoes, skordalia, and lemon wedges.

Hearty Italian lentil and vegetable soup

VEGETARIAN | PREP + COOK TIME **50 MINUTES** | SERVES **4**

While meaty stews are often the comfort food of choice when the weather gets chilly,
a big bowl of lentil soup is a great vegetarian substitute. Lentils have the second-highest
ratio of protein per kilojoules of any legume, after soybeans, and are rich in folate,
vitamin B6, and iron.

1 tbsp extra virgin olive oil

1 medium onion (150g), finely chopped

3 garlic cloves, crushed

2 tsp finely grated fresh ginger

1 tsp cumin seeds, lightly crushed

1 fresh long red chilli, finely chopped

1 medium carrot (120g), finely chopped

2 trimmed celery stalks (200g), finely chopped

2 fresh bay leaves

3 fresh thyme sprigs, plus extra to serve

1¼ cups (185g) dried French-style green lentils, rinsed

¼ cup (70g) tomato paste

6 cups (1.5 litres) vegetable stock

1½ tbsp lemon juice

salt and freshly ground black pepper

⅓ cup (25g) finely grated parmesan

1 fresh long red chilli, extra, thinly sliced

1 Heat the olive oil in a large saucepan over a medium-high heat; cook the onion, garlic, ginger, cumin, long chilli, carrot, and celery, stirring, for 10 minutes or until the vegetables are softened.

2 Add the bay leaves, thyme, lentils, tomato paste, and stock, bring to the boil; reduce heat to low. Cook for 20 minutes or until the lentils are tender. Stir in the lemon juice; season with salt and pepper to taste.

3 Ladle the soup into bowls, top with the parmesan and extra chilli. Sprinkle with extra thyme before serving, if you like.

Salmon parcels with kipfler potatoes

PESCATARIAN | PREP + COOK TIME **50 MINUTES** | SERVES **2**

After tuna, salmon might be the most popular fish in the world to eat. Luckily when baked, pan-fried, or grilled, salmon is also among the most heart-healthy of fish. It is packed with vitamins and minerals, such as B12, vitamin D, and selenium, and is a good source of niacin, omega-3 fatty acids, protein, phosphorus, and potassium.

300g kipfler (fingerling) potatoes, thinly sliced

1 small red onion (100g), cut into thin wedges

1 tbsp extra virgin olive oil

1/2 medium lemon (70g), thinly sliced

1 small tomato (90g), thinly sliced

2 x 180g skinless boneless salmon fillets

2 tsp capers

1 tsp fennel seeds

100g baby spinach leaves

1/4 cup (15g) fresh flat-leaf parsley leaves

1 Preheat oven to 200°C (180°C fan/400°F/Gas 6).

2 Combine the potato and onion in a roasting pan; drizzle with half the olive oil. Roast for 30 minutes or until lightly browned and tender.

3 Meanwhile, arrange the lemon and tomato on two 30cm square pieces of baking paper. Top with the salmon, capers, and fennel seeds; drizzle with the remaining olive oil. Fold the paper into a parcel to enclose the salmon; place on an oven tray. Bake for 8 minutes or until the salmon is cooked as desired.

4 Serve the salmon parcels with the potato and onion; top with spinach and parsley.

TIPS

- Baking the salmon in a parcel locks in all the flavours, juices, and steam to give a moist and flavoursome result. The cooking time will vary depending on the thickness of the cut.
- You could try using firm white fish fillets or even chicken breast instead of salmon.

Cheese and silverbeet borek with crunchy seeds

VEGETARIAN | PREP + COOK TIME **1 HOUR 20 MINUTES** | SERVES **6**

Silverbeet, sometimes mistakenly called spinach in greengrocers, is also known as Swiss chard to further confuse the issue. One thing for certain, however, is that it should be used in this recipe rather than spinach, for its stronger flavour and hardier texture, and because its leaves contain far less water than spinach the pastry is more likely to stay crisp.

6 large stalks silverbeet (Swiss chard) (480g)

5 eggs

500g firm ricotta cheese (see tip)

200g Greek feta, crumbled

1 cup (240g) sour cream

1/2 cup (180ml) soda water

salt and freshly ground black pepper

290g filo pastry

olive oil cooking spray

1 tsp poppy seeds

1 tbsp sunflower seeds

1 tbsp pepitas (pumpkin seeds)

Greek yogurt, to serve

1 medium lemon (140g), cut into wedges

TIP

Fresh firm ricotta purchased from a deli is best for this recipe.

1 Preheat oven to 180°C (160°C fan/350°F/Gas 4). Oil and line a 22cm x 32cm, 6cm deep ovenproof dish with baking paper, extending the paper 2cm over the sides.

2 Trim 4cm from the silverbeet stems; separate the leaves and stems. Finely shred the leaves; finely chop the stems. You will need 4 cups (180g) shredded leaves and 1½ cups (200g) finely chopped stems.

3 Heat a lightly oiled large frying pan over a high heat; cook the silverbeet leaves and stems for 2 minutes or until wilted and tender. When cool enough to handle, squeeze the excess liquid from the silverbeet; set aside to cool.

4 Whisk 4 of the eggs in a large bowl until combined. Add the ricotta, feta, sour cream, soda water, and silverbeet, stir to combine; season with salt and pepper.

5 Layer five sheets of the filo pastry, spraying each sheet with oil; place on the bottom of the dish, trimming to fit. Keep the remaining sheets covered with baking paper topped with a clean, damp tea towel to prevent them from drying out. Pour a quarter of the cheese mixture onto the pastry.

6 Layer two sheets of pastry, spraying each sheet with oil; place on top of the cheese mixture. Pour another quarter of the cheese mixture onto the pastry. Repeat layering with two more layers of pastry and the remaining cheese mixture. Layer five sheets of pastry, spraying each sheet with oil; place on top of the cheese mixture and tuck the edges in.

7 Whisk the remaining egg lightly; brush over the top of the pie. Sprinkle the pie with the combined seeds; bake for 40 minutes or until golden and cooked through.

8 Serve the pie with Greek yogurt and lemon wedges.

WEEKEND ENTERTAINING

Stunning fresh ingredients and classic
Mediterranean flavours give these dishes the
wow factor, sure to add finesse to a dinner
party menu or a casual dinner with friends.

Gazpacho with feta and prawns

PESCATARIAN | PREP + COOK TIME **20 MINUTES** | SERVES **6**

The word gazpacho is derived from the Arabic for "soaked bread". It is a cold soup from southern Spain, made by blending raw vegetables. Gazpacho is traditionally served with accompaniments such as croutons, additional chopped vegetables, and chopped egg for diners to add as they wish. This luxurious version is instead topped with prawns and feta.

8 medium tomatoes (1.2kg), coarsely chopped

2 medium red capsicums (peppers) (400g), coarsely chopped

2 medium cucumbers (260g), peeled, coarsely chopped

1 small onion (80g), coarsely chopped

3 garlic cloves, crushed

160g sourdough bread, coarsely chopped

1¼ cups (300ml) extra virgin olive oil

½ cup (125ml) red wine vinegar

1 cup (250ml) water

salt and freshly ground black pepper

1kg cooked medium king prawns

4 slices sourdough bread (200g), extra, crusts removed

160g Greek feta, crumbled

2 tbsp small fresh oregano leaves

1 Blend the tomato, capsicum, cucumber, onion, garlic, bread, 1 cup (240ml) of the olive oil, the vinegar, and the water for 3 minutes or until smooth. Season with salt and pepper to taste.

2 Shell and devein the prawns, leaving the tails intact.

3 Tear the extra sourdough into coarse pieces. Heat 2 tablespoons of the olive oil in a large frying pan over a medium-high heat. Cook the bread, stirring frequently, for 2 minutes or until the croûtons are golden.

4 Ladle the soup into serving bowls; top with the croûtons, feta, prawns, and oregano leaves. Drizzle the soup with the remaining oil.

TIP

Use the ripest tomatoes you can find to maximize the flavour of this classic Spanish soup.

Chicken skewers with peach caprese salad

PREP + COOK TIME **25 MINUTES** | SERVES **4**

A traditional Caprese salad, delicious in its simplicity, is comprised of layers of sliced fresh mozzarella, basil, and luscious sun-ripened tomatoes. Traditionally served as an antipasto, here we have made our caprese a little more substantial with the addition of grilled chicken skewers and peach cheeks, which complement the richness of the buffalo mozzarella.

400g chicken breast fillets, cut into 2cm pieces

1¹/₂ tbsp extra virgin olive oil (see tips)

salt and freshly ground black pepper

4 medium peaches (600g)

250g buffalo mozzarella, torn (see tips)

2 medium tomatoes (300g), sliced

400g mixed heirloom cherry tomatoes, halved, quartered if large (see tips)

¹/₂ cup fresh small basil leaves

1 tbsp white wine vinegar

pistachio mint pesto

¹/₂ cup (70g) pistachios

1¹/₂ cups (75g) fresh mint leaves

1 cup (60g) fresh flat-leaf parsley leaves

1 garlic clove, crushed

2 tsp finely grated lemon rind

2 tsp lemon juice

¹/₂ cup (125ml) extra virgin olive oil

1 Make the pistachio mint pesto. Blend or process the ingredients until smooth; season with salt and pepper to taste.

2 Cut the sides off the peaches in fat slices, cutting as close to the pit as possible. Discard the pits.

3 Combine the chicken and 1 tablespoon of the olive oil in a medium bowl; season with salt and pepper. Thread onto four skewers.

4 Cook the chicken on a heated oiled grill plate (or pan or barbecue) for 8 minutes. Add the peaches to the grill plate; cook for a further 2 minutes or until the chicken is cooked through and the peaches are golden.

5 Layer the grilled peaches with the mozzarella, tomatoes, and basil; drizzle with the vinegar and remaining olive oil. Serve the salad topped with the chicken and pesto.

TIPS

- You can use chilli-infused olive oil for marinating the chicken, if you like.
- Buffalo mozzarella has a tangier flavour than cow's milk mozzarella, which may be used instead.
- Swap heirloom tomatoes for regular cherry tomatoes, if preferred.

Fish with pine nuts, currants, and cavolo nero

PESCATARIAN | PREP + COOK TIME **25 MINUTES** | SERVES **4**

This agro dolce (sweet and sour) Italian recipe uses currants and grapes for sweetness and vinegar for a sour note. Grapes contain powerful antioxidants known as polyphenols, which may slow or prevent many types of cancer. The resveratrol found in red wine famous for heart health is a type of polyphenol present in the skins of red grapes.

$1/3$ cup (80ml) extra virgin olive oil

1 medium red onion (170g), halved, sliced thinly

1 cup (170g) small red grapes, halved if large

2 tbsp currants

300g cavolo nero (tuscan cabbage), trimmed, coarsely chopped

$1/4$ cup (60ml) red wine vinegar

$1/3$ cup (50g) pine nuts, toasted

8 skinless, boneless firm white fish fillets (800g) (see tip)

fresh flat-leaf parsley sprigs, to serve

1 Heat $1/4$ cup (60ml) of the oil in a large deep frying pan over medium-high heat; cook onion for 4 minutes or until softened. Add grapes and currants; cook for 1 minute. Add cavolo nero and vinegar; cook, stirring, for 1 minute or until cavolo nero just wilts. Add pine nuts.

2 Heat remaining oil in a large frying pan over medium-high heat; cook fish, in two batches, for $1^{1/2}$ minutes on each side or until just cooked through.

3 Serve fish with cavolo nero mixture, sprinkled with parsley.

TIP

You can use any white-fleshed fish, such as bass, halibut, whiting, or john dory.

Chilli sardine pasta with pine nuts and currants

PESCATARIAN | PREP + COOK TIME **20 MINUTES** | SERVES **4**

Dried fruits have long been an important component of the Mediterranean diet, eaten on their own or in traditional dishes. True currants are from the region of Corinth, and are small and black with an intense sweet flavour. Greece is still the primary producer of currants, with about 80 per cent of total world production coming from the country.

400g spaghetti

$1/3$ cup (80ml) extra virgin olive oil

2 x 120g cans sardines in lemon, chilli, and garlic oil (see tips)

$1/4$ cup (40g) pine nuts, toasted

$1/4$ cup (40g) currants

2 tbsp lemon juice

salt and freshly ground black pepper

2 tsp finely grated lemon rind

$1/2$ cup (30g) fresh flat-leaf parsley leaves, coarsely chopped

120g rocket leaves

1 baby fennel bulb (130g), trimmed, thinly sliced (see tips)

lemon wedges, to serve

1 Cook the pasta in a large saucepan of boiling salted water until almost tender; drain, reserving 1 cup (240ml) of the cooking water.

2 Meanwhile, heat $1/4$ cup of the olive oil in a large frying pan over a medium heat. Add the sardines; cook, stirring occasionally, for 2 minutes or until heated through.

3 Add the pasta, pine nuts, currants, and lemon juice to the sardines. Heat pan over a high heat. Add enough reserved water to moisten the pasta; cook, stirring, for 2 minutes. Season with salt and pepper to taste.

4 Combine the lemon rind and parsley in a small bowl; stir half through the pasta.

5 Place the rocket and fennel in a bowl.

6 Divide the pasta among four bowls; sprinkle with the remaining lemon rind mixture and drizzle with the remaining olive oil. Serve with the rocket and fennel salad and lemon wedges.

TIPS

- Sardines in flavoured oils are available from major supermarkets and delicatessens.
- Use a mandoline or V-slicer to slice the fennel very thinly.

Lamb, spinach, and feta pie

PREP + COOK TIME **1 HOUR 20 MINUTES + STANDING** | SERVES **6**

The filling for this pie is quintessentially Greek with its flavoursome tomato-based lamb sauce. For individual pies, spoon the filling mixture into six 1-cup (250ml) ovenproof dishes. Cut the pastry into smaller rectangles; place slightly overlapping to cover the filling. Keep an eye on the pastry while baking as the cooking time will differ from the large pie.

$^1/_4$ cup (60ml) extra virgin olive oil

2 medium onions (300g), finely chopped

3 trimmed celery stalks (450g), finely chopped

4 garlic cloves, crushed

1kg minced lamb

$^1/_2$ cup (125ml) dry red wine

$1^1/_2$ cups (375ml) vegetable stock

2 x 400g can chopped tomatoes

$^1/_3$ cup (95g) tomato paste

1 tbsp chopped fresh oregano leaves

2 cinnamon sticks

150g Greek feta, crumbled

100g baby spinach leaves

salt and freshly ground black pepper

2 sheets frozen shortcrust pastry, thawed slightly

1 egg

1 egg yolk

1 tsp sea salt flakes

1 tsp fennel seeds

1 Preheat oven to 220°C (200°C fan/425°F/Gas 7).

2 Heat the olive oil in a large frying pan over a medium heat; cook the onion and celery, stirring, for 5 minutes or until lightly browned. Add the garlic; cook for 1 minute.

3 Increase heat to high, add the lamb; cook, stirring, until browned, breaking it up with the back of a wooden spoon. Add the wine; cook for 2 minutes. Add the stock, tomatoes, tomato paste, oregano, and cinnamon; cook for 35 minutes or until the liquid is evaporated and the sauce is thick. Cool.

4 Stir the feta and spinach into the lamb mixture, season with salt and pepper to taste; spoon into a 20cm round pie tin or 6-cup (1.5-litre) ovenproof dish.

5 Cut each sheet of pastry into ten equal rectangles. Place the pastry rectangles on top, slightly overlapping to cover the filling. Brush the pastry with the combined beaten egg and egg yolk; sprinkle with salt and the fennel seeds.

6 Bake the pie for 25 minutes or until the pastry is a deep golden; cover the pastry with pieces of foil if it starts to over brown. Stand for 10 minutes before serving.

TIP

The spinach can be replaced with silverbeet (Swiss chard) or even kale if you prefer; simply discard the tough centre stalks first.

Spicy prawn and white bean panzanella

PESCATARIAN | PREP + COOK TIME **20 MINUTES** | SERVES **4**

Before the advent of modern supermarket bread, every cuisine around the world had a recipe for using stale bread – panzanella is Italy's answer to this age-old problem. While starting off as a simple peasant dish born of necessity, panzanella has long been a dish favoured for its simplicity that allows the flavours of good-quality ingredients to shine through.

160g wholegrain sourdough bread

olive oil cooking spray

1 medium lemon (140g)

800g cooked medium king prawns

400g can cannellini beans, drained, rinsed

250g mixed cherry tomatoes, halved

2 medium cucumbers (260g), chopped

1 small red onion (100g), thinly sliced

1/2 cup (60g) pitted Sicilian olives, halved

1 fresh long red chilli, thinly sliced

1 cup (20g) fresh basil leaves

120g soft goat's cheese, crumbled

1/4 cup (60ml) extra virgin olive oil

1/3 cup (80ml) red wine vinegar

1 garlic clove, crushed

salt and freshly ground black pepper

1 Preheat oven to 220°C (200°C fan/425°F/Gas 7). Line a large oven tray with baking paper.

2 Tear the bread coarsely into bite-sized pieces, place on the lined tray; spray with oil. Bake for 5 minutes or until golden and crisp.

3 Remove the rind from the lemon in long thin strips using a zester (see tips). Shell and devein the prawns, leaving the tails intact.

4 Place the bread, lemon rind, prawns, beans, tomatoes, cucumber, onion, olives, chilli, basil, and half the goat's cheese in a large bowl; toss gently to combine.

5 Combine the olive oil, vinegar, and garlic in a small bowl; season with salt and pepper to taste. Just before serving, spoon the dressing over the salad; top with the remaining cheese.

TIPS

- If you don't have a zester, you can finely grate the lemon rind instead.
- You could use marinated feta instead of goat's cheese.
- If you like, omit the prawns and add a can of flaked drained tuna in olive oil.

Spanish-style fish with smoky aubergine

PESCATARIAN | PREP + COOK TIME **55 MINUTES + STANDING** | SERVES **4**

Red mullet is a fish particularly favoured in Mediterranean cuisine for its delicate flavour and beautiful colour. Aubergine is rich in anthocyanins, flavonoids that reduce blood pressure and lower risk of cardiovascular disease. It also possesses an abundance of nasunin, an antioxidant, in its bright purple skin.

4 small aubergines (400g)

1 medium red capsicum (pepper) (200g)

salt and freshly ground black pepper

1 tsp smoked paprika

2 tbsp extra virgin olive oil

12 red mullet fillets (960g), skin on (see tip)

400g can cannellini beans, drained, rinsed

½ cup (150g) whole-egg mayonnaise

1 garlic clove, crushed

1 tbsp lemon juice

¼ cup (15g) fresh flat-leaf parsley leaves

lemon cheeks, to serve

1. Preheat oven to 200°C (180°C fan/400°F/Gas 6). Line an oven tray with baking paper.

2. Cut the aubergines in half lengthways; score flesh at 1cm intervals. Quarter the capsicum; discard seeds and membranes. Place the aubergine and capsicum, skin-side up, on the lined tray. Roast for 30 minutes or until the capsicum skin blisters and blackens and the aubergine is tender. Transfer to a heatproof bowl; cover for 5 minutes. Peel away the vegetable skins. Shred the aubergine coarsely; slice the capsicum thickly. Season with salt and pepper to taste.

3. Meanwhile, combine the smoked paprika and half the olive oil in a medium shallow bowl, add the fish; turn to coat. Heat a large non-stick frying pan over a high heat; cook the fish, in two batches, skin-side first, for 1½ minutes each side or until just cooked through. Transfer to a plate; stand, covered loosely with foil.

4. Meanwhile, heat the remaining olive oil in the same pan over a medium heat; cook the beans, stirring, until warmed through. Season with salt and pepper to taste.

5. Meanwhile, combine the mayonnaise, garlic, and lemon juice in a small bowl to make aïoli; season with salt and pepper to taste.

6. Combine the aubergine, capsicum, and beans; top with the fish and parsley. Serve with the aïoli and lemon cheeks.

TIP

Use butterflied sardine fillets or other white fish fillets instead of red mullet, if you like.

Lamb with spinach pesto dressing

PREP + COOK TIME **35 MINUTES** | SERVES **4**

While we often think first of nuts, seeds, and oily fish as the greatest suppliers of omega-3 fats, lamb is also a great source of these fatty acids. It is also provides protein and vital nutrients like iron, zinc, selenium, and vitamin B12. Whenever possible, buy locally produced or grass-fed lamb, which packs an extra nutritional punch while benefiting local producers.

600g lamb backstraps (eye of loin)

1 garlic clove, crushed

salt and freshly ground black pepper

1 tbsp extra virgin olive oil

1 small red onion (100g), cut into thin wedges

3 medium heirloom tomatoes (450g), quartered

25g rocket leaves

$^1/_2$ cup (100g) marinated soft goat's cheese, reserve 2 tbsp of the marinating oil (see tips)

spinach pesto dressing

$^1/_2$ cup (130g) baby spinach pesto (see tips)

$^1/_4$ cup (60ml) extra virgin olive oil

1 Combine the lamb, garlic, and olive oil in a medium bowl; season with salt and pepper.

2 Cook the onion on a heated oiled grill plate (or pan or barbecue) until browned and just tender; season with salt and pepper to taste. Cover loosely with foil to keep warm.

3 Cook the lamb on the heated oiled grill plate (or pan or barbecue), turning occasionally, for 10 minutes for medium or until cooked as desired. Stand, covered loosely with foil, for 5 minutes. Slice thickly.

4 Meanwhile, to make the spinach pesto dressing, place the ingredients in a small screw-top jar; shake well. Season with salt and pepper to taste.

5 Place the onion, tomato, rocket, and reserved marinating oil in a large bowl; toss gently to combine. Season with salt and pepper to taste.

6 Add the lamb to the salad; toss to combine. Arrange salad on a platter. Top with the crumbled cheese; drizzle with the dressing.

TIPS

- The oil from the marinated goat's cheese adds extra depth of flavour to this dish. The cheese we used was marinated in a mixture of olive oil, garlic, thyme, and chilli.
- If you've made your own pesto, use this instead of baby spinach pesto, if you like, or swap with your favourite store-bought pesto.

Pan-fried fish with tomato and olive salsa

PESCATARIAN | PREP + COOK TIME **50 MINUTES** | SERVES **6**

Eating a wide variety of seafood has a range of health benefits. Fish contain a large array of vitamins and minerals including vitamins A and D, phosphorus, magnesium, and selenium. Omega-3 fatty acids, found abundantly in seafood, are essential for our healthy development, and have been shown to help protect against heart disease and strokes.

1kg kipfler (fingerling) potatoes, halved lengthways

2 tbsp red wine vinegar

$1/4$ cup (60ml) extra virgin olive oil

400g green beans, trimmed

$1/2$ cup (75g) plain flour

salt and freshly ground black pepper

12 x 80g white fish fillets, skin on

lemon wedges, to serve

tomato and olive salsa

$1/3$ cup (80ml) extra virgin olive oil

2 garlic cloves, crushed

500g grape (cherry) tomatoes, halved

150g pitted Kalamata olives, halved

$1/2$ small red onion (50g), finely chopped

$1/2$ cup fresh flat-leaf parsley leaves

2 tbsp lemon juice

1. Make the tomato and olive salsa. Heat 1 tablespoon of olive oil in a medium saucepan over a medium heat; cook the garlic, stirring, until fragrant. Stir in the tomatoes and olives; cook until heated through. Remove from heat; stir in the onion, parsley, remaining olive oil, and the lemon juice. Season with salt and pepper to taste.

2. Place the potatoes in a large saucepan, cover with cold water; bring to the boil. Boil for 8 minutes or until tender; drain. Transfer to a large bowl; drizzle with the vinegar and 1 tablespoon of the oil. Cover to keep warm.

3. Meanwhile, cook the green beans in a saucepan of boiling water for 3 minutes or until tender; drain. Refresh in a bowl of iced water; drain. Add to the potatoes in the bowl; toss gently to combine.

4. Season the flour with salt and pepper; coat the fish in the seasoned flour, shake off excess. Heat the remaining olive oil in a large frying pan over a medium heat; cook fish, skin-side down, in batches, for $1^{1/2}$ minutes or until skin crisps. Turn, cook for a further 1 minute or until the fish is just cooked through.

5. Divide the potato and beans among plates; top with the fish and salsa. Serve with lemon wedges.

TIP

The salsa can be partially prepared up to a day ahead; add the parsley, remaining oil, and lemon juice just before you cook the fish.

Barbecued calamari with lemon cracked wheat risotto

PESCATARIAN | PREP + COOK TIME **45 MINUTES** | SERVES **2**

Bulgur is used extensively in Middle Eastern cuisine, but is also enjoyed throughout the Mediterranean region. Eaten as you would rice or couscous, bulgur has a course texture and nutty flavour, and can be used in soups, stews, and salads. Bulgur is low in fat, high in minerals and iron, plus is a good source of plant-based protein.

300g cleaned small calamari hoods, halved lengthways (see tips)

3 garlic cloves, crushed

2 tsp chopped fresh oregano leaves

1 tsp finely grated lemon rind

1 tbsp extra virgin olive oil

1 small onion, finely chopped

2 tsp fresh lemon thyme leaves

1/2 cup (100g) coarse bulgur (bulgur wheat)

2 cups (500ml) water

1 cup (140g) frozen peas

1 tbsp lemon juice

2 tsp fresh oregano leaves, extra

1 Using a sharp knife, score the inside surface of the calamari in a criss-cross pattern at 1cm intervals. Cut into 4cm strips. Place in a bowl with 1 garlic clove, the chopped oregano, lemon rind, and 2 teaspoons of the olive oil; stir to combine.

2 Heat the remaining olive oil in a medium non-stick frying pan over a medium heat; cook the onion, remaining garlic, and thyme, stirring, for 5 minutes or until the onion is softened.

3 Add the bulgur and the water; cook, stirring occasionally, for 15 minutes or until the bulgur is tender. Add the peas and lemon juice; cook, stirring, for 2 minutes or until heated through.

4 Meanwhile, cook the calamari on a heated grill plate (or pan or barbecue), turning halfway through the cooking time, for 2 minutes or until just cooked through.

5 Serve the calamari with the bulgur mixture; sprinkle with the extra oregano.

TIPS

- If you want to clean your own calamari you will need 850g whole calamari.
- You could also try this recipe with thin strips of chicken or pork.

Fennel

Fennel is a flowering plant species in the carrot family. Grown for its edible bulbs, shoots, leaves, and seeds it is used extensively in Mediterranean cooking. Aromatic and flavoursome it's also a rich source of fibre, protein, minerals, and B vitamins.

Maple-roasted fennel

VEGAN | PREP + COOK TIME **35 MINUTES** | SERVES **4**

Preheat oven to 200°C (180°C fan/400°F/Gas 6). Reserve the green fennel fronds from 4 baby (520g) fennel bulbs. Cut the fennel bulbs in half; place on a baking-paper-lined oven tray. Add 8 fresh thyme sprigs and 2 tablespoons each of pure maple syrup and olive oil; toss to combine, turn the fennel cut-side down. Season with salt and pepper. Roast for 25 minutes or until tender and browned. Serve the fennel drizzled with balsamic vinegar, topped with the reserved fronds and 1/4 cup (40g) roasted flaked almonds.

Shaved fennel slaw

VEGAN | PREP TIME **15 MINUTES** | SERVES **4**

Place 350g shredded white cabbage in a large bowl with 1 medium (300g) thinly shaved fennel bulb, 1 thinly sliced seeded green chilli, 1 cup each of fresh coriander (16g) and fresh mint leaves (50g); toss gently to combine. Combine 1/4 cup (60ml) each of lemon juice and extra virgin olive oil in a small bowl; season with salt and pepper to taste. Drizzle the dressing over the slaw; toss gently to combine.

Pickled fennel bruschetta

VEGETARIAN | PREP + COOK TIME **15 MINUTES + STANDING** SERVES **4**

Place 1 small (200g) thinly sliced fennel bulb in a medium bowl with 1 crushed garlic clove, 1/3 cup (80ml) white balsamic vinegar, 2 teaspoons of caster sugar, and 6 thinly sliced red radishes; toss to combine. Stand for 30 minutes. Drain. Spread 180g drained Persian feta on 4 slices of char-grilled sourdough bread; top with the pickled fennel.

Grapefruit and fennel salad

VEGAN | PREP TIME **15 MINUTES** | SERVES **4**

Cut 1 pink grapefruit (350g) into segments. Place the grapefruit in a medium bowl with 1 medium (300g) thinly shaved fennel bulb and 1/4 cup squashed Sicilian olives; toss gently to combine. Whisk 1/4 cup (60ml) grapefruit juice, 1 crushed garlic clove, 1 1/2 tablespoons of sherry vinegar and 2 tablespoons of olive oil in a small bowl. Serve the salad drizzled with the dressing.

CLOCKWISE from top left

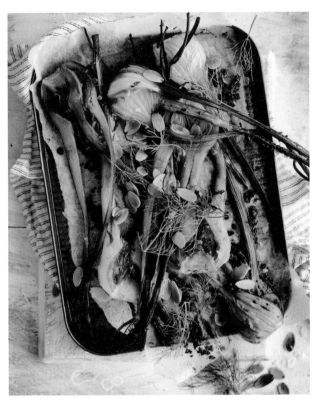

Lamb kofta with courgette baba ganoush

PREP + COOK TIME **1 HOUR 15 MINUTES + REFRIGERATION** | SERVES **4**

Traditionally baba ganoush is a dish consisting of a mixture of smoky aubergine, tahini, olive oil, and various spices. In our version we have replaced the aubergine with roasted courgette for a lighter twist on the classic. Tahini is a paste made from toasted hulled sesame seeds and is available from most major supermarkets and Middle Eastern food stores.

600g boneless lamb leg meat, coarsely chopped

1 egg

2 tsp ground cumin

1 garlic clove, crushed

$^3/_4$ cup (36g) finely chopped fresh mint leaves

salt and freshly ground black pepper

1 medium lemon (140g)

1 cup (200g) pearl barley

3 cups (750ml) water

$1^1/_2$ cups (180g) frozen peas

$^1/_3$ cup (80ml) extra virgin olive oil

mint leaves, extra, to serve

courgette baba ganoush

2 large courgettes (300g), untrimmed

$1^1/_2$ tbsp extra virgin olive oil

1 tbsp tahini

$^1/_2$ tsp ground cumin

1 small garlic clove, crushed

TIP

Chilling the food processor bowl and blade in the freezer for 15 minutes before processing the kofta mixture ensures the mixture is nicely chopped and not mushy.

1 Process the lamb, egg, cumin, and garlic in a food processor until finely chopped. Place in a large bowl with $^1/_4$ cup (12g) of chopped mint. Season with salt and pepper and knead for 2 minutes or until well combined. Divide the mixture into 8 portions. Shape the portions into koftas. Press onto skewers. Refrigerate for 1 hour.

2 Meanwhile, finely grate the rind from a lemon. Squeeze the juice; reserve $1^1/_2$ tablespoons of juice for the baba ganoush.

3 To make the courgette baba ganoush, preheat oven to 220°C (200°C fan/425°F/Gas 7). Bake the whole courgettes on an oven tray for 40 minutes or until very soft and slightly blackened. Process the courgette with the olive oil, tahini, cumin, garlic, and reserved lemon juice. Season with salt and pepper to taste.

4 Place the pearl barley and the water in a medium saucepan, bring to the boil. Reduce heat to low; cook, covered, for 35 minutes or until tender. Drain. Cook the peas in a saucepan of boiling water for 2 minutes or until tender; drain.

5 Place the pearl barley, peas, lemon rind, remaining chopped mint, and 2 tablespoons of olive oil in a large bowl; toss gently to combine. Season with salt and pepper to taste.

6 Brush the kofta with the remaining olive oil; cook on a heated grill plate (or barbecue) over a medium-high heat, turning, for 10 minutes or until cooked as desired.

7 Serve the kofta with the baba ganoush and pearl barley salad, sprinkled with mint.

Roasted fish with celeriac and fennel salad

PESCATARIAN | PREP + COOK TIME **1 HOUR + REFRIGERATION AND STANDING** | SERVES **8**

Roasting a whole fish may seem intimidating, but there really is nothing to it, and they make an amazing impression when plated and served. Juniper berries are not true berries, but are seeds produced by the various species of juniper trees. Used as a spice in European cuisine, they also give gin its distinctive flavour. They are the only spice to be derived from conifers.

8 whole small white fish (2.6kg), cleaned (see tips)

salt and freshly ground black pepper

8 thyme sprigs, trimmed

2 garlic cloves, thinly sliced

1 tbsp dried juniper berries

1/4 cup (60ml) extra virgin olive oil

1 tbsp finely grated lemon rind or strips

lemon cheeks, to serve

celeriac and fennel salad

700g celeriac, peeled, cut into fine matchsticks (see tips)

2 small fennel bulbs (400g), trimmed, thinly sliced (see tips), fronds reserved

1/3 cup (20g) fresh flat-leaf parsley leaves

1/3 cup (80ml) lemon juice

1/4 cup (60ml) extra virgin olive oil

1 Wash the fish inside and out, pat dry with paper towel. Season inside and out with salt and pepper. Score the fish three times through the thickest part on both sides. Place on an oven tray. Place a thyme sprig, some reserved fennel fronds, and a slice of garlic into each cut. Using a mortar and pestle, grind the juniper berries into a coarse powder. Coat the fish all over with half the olive oil, the lemon rind, and the ground juniper berries. Refrigerate for 1 hour.

2 Meanwhile, to make the celeriac and fennel salad, combine the ingredients in a large bowl; season with salt and pepper to taste.

3 Preheat oven to 180°C (160°C fan/350°F/Gas 4). Line a large oven tray with baking paper.

4 Brush the fish with the remaining olive oil; place on the lined oven tray. Roast the fish for 18 minutes or until cooked through. Stand, covered loosely with foil, for 5 minutes.

5 Serve the fish with the salad and lemon cheeks.

TIPS

- You can use any small white fish that you prefer. Speak to your fish monger and see what is local and in season.
- Use a mandoline or V-slicer to quickly and easily cut the celeriac into fine matchsticks and the fennel into thin slices.

Seafood and saffron stew

PESCATARIAN | PREP + COOK TIME **1 HOUR** | SERVES **4**

A long held misconception is that if a mussel does not open when cooked, it should be discarded as it is "bad". This is a myth. As the molluscs are cooked, the heat softens the muscles that keep the shell together. If a mussel doesn't open during cooking, it is because the muscle hasn't softened sufficiently, but the mussel is actually fine to eat.

4 cleaned baby calamari hoods (480g) (see tips)

250g small black mussels (see tips)

1 tbsp extra virgin olive oil

2 medium onions (300g), finely chopped

2 garlic cloves, crushed

3 wide strips orange rind (see tips)

1 fresh long red chilli, finely chopped

pinch of saffron threads

1/3 cup (80ml) dry white wine

2 x 400g can chopped tomatoes

4 cups (1 litre) fish stock

1kg uncooked large king prawns, peeled, deveined, with tails intact

200g pippis (clams), scrubbed

200g baby octopus, cleaned

2 baby fennel bulbs (260g)

2 tbsp lemon juice

1 Using a sharp knife, slice the calamari hoods crossways into 1cm rings. Scrub the mussels; remove beards.

2 Heat the olive oil in a large saucepan; cook the onion, stirring, until soft. Add the garlic; cook, stirring, for 1 minute.

3 Add the orange rind, chilli, saffron, and wine to the onion mixture; cook, stirring, for 2 minutes. Add the tomatoes; cook for 10 minutes or until the mixture thickens slightly. Add the stock; cook for 20 minutes or until the liquid is reduced by about a quarter.

4 Add the calamari, prawns, cleaned mussels, clams, and octopus to the pan. Cook, covered, stirring occasionally, for 5 minutes or until the seafood is just cooked.

5 Meanwhile, trim the fennel; reserve fronds. Using a mandoline or V-slicer, cut the fennel into very thin slices. Place the fennel and lemon juice in a small bowl; toss to coat well.

6 Serve stew topped with the fennel mixture and reserved fennel fronds.

TIPS

- If you want to clean your own calamari you will need 4 whole calamari.
- Discard mussels that open before cooking and smell bad.
- For wide orange strips, use a vegetable peeler to peel strips and avoid taking off too much of the white pith with the rind as it is bitter.

Roasted rosemary pork, fennel, and potatoes

PREP + COOK TIME **1 HOUR 15 MINUTES + STANDING** | SERVES **4**

Fennel is a crunchy green vegetable that's eaten raw in salads; fried as an accompaniment; or used as an ingredient in soups and sauces. It is also the name given to the dried seeds of the plant, which have a stronger liquorice flavour. The Greek name for fennel is *marathon* and the place of the famous battle of Marathon literally means a plain with fennel.

1 tbsp finely chopped fresh rosemary leaves

2 tsp finely chopped fresh oregano leaves

2 tsp fennel seeds

1/2 tsp dried chilli flakes

1/3 cup (80ml) extra virgin olive oil

salt and freshly ground black pepper

4 small fennel bulbs (800g), trimmed, quartered

800g kipfler (fingerling) potatoes, halved lengthways

500g pork fillet

lemon wedges, to serve

1 Preheat oven to 220°C (200°C fan/425°F/Gas 7).

2 Combine the rosemary, oregano, fennel seeds, chilli, and 1/4 cup (60ml) of the olive oil in a small bowl; season with salt and pepper. Place the fennel bulbs and potato in a large roasting pan. Drizzle with two-thirds of the rosemary mixture; toss to combine. Roast for 30 minutes.

3 Rub the pork with the remaining rosemary mixture. Heat the remaining olive oil in a heavy-based frying pan over a high heat. Add the pork; cook, turning, for 5 minutes or until browned all over.

4 Stir the potato and fennel bulbs; place the pork on top of the vegetables. Roast for 20 minutes or until pork is just cooked through. Stand the pork, covered loosely with foil, for 5 minutes.

5 Cut the pork into slices; serve with the potato, fennel, and lemon wedges.

TIPS

- You could replace the pork with chicken breasts.
- Sprinkle with fennel fronds and fresh oregano leaves before serving, if you like.

Mussels in chilli broth with freekeh

PESCATARIAN | PREP + COOK TIME **1 HOUR 35 MINUTES** | SERVES **4**

Mussels, like most seafood, are high in omega-3 fatty acids, which have been linked to a wide variety of health benefits such as a decreased risk of cancer and cardiovascular disease, the reduction of inflammatory conditions, such as arthritis, and improving brain function. They are also relatively low in calories and fat, while high in protein, vitamins, and minerals.

1kg black mussels (see tips)

1 cup (250ml) dry white wine

1 tbsp extra virgin olive oil

1 medium onion (150g), finely chopped

2 stalks celery (300g), trimmed, halved lengthways, thinly sliced

400g baby carrots, trimmed, thinly sliced on the diagonal

2 tbsp tomato paste

1 cup (170g) wholegrain green-wheat freekeh (see tips)

$\frac{1}{2}$ tsp dried chilli flakes

3 cups (750ml) fish stock

coarsely chopped fresh flat-leaf parsley, to serve

lemon wedges, to serve

1 Scrub the mussels; remove beards.

2 Bring the wine to the boil in a large saucepan over a medium-high heat. Add the mussels; cook, covered, for 8 minutes or until the mussels open (see tips). Drain the mussels in a colander over a large heatproof bowl; reserve the cooking liquid. Cover the mussels loosely with foil to keep them warm.

3 Heat the olive oil in the same pan over a medium heat; cook the onion, celery, and carrot for 3 minutes or until the onion softens. Add the tomato paste, freekeh, and chilli flakes; cook, stirring, for 1 minute or until fragrant. Add the stock and reserved cooking liquid; bring to the boil. Reduce heat to low; cook, partially covered, for 1 hour until the freekeh is tender.

4 Add the mussels to the pan; cook for 2 minutes or until heated through.

5 Top the mussel and freekeh mixture with parsley; serve with lemon wedges.

TIP

- Some mussels might not open after cooking; these might need careful prompting with a knife.
- Freekeh is an ancient grain food made from roasted young green wheat; it is available at health food shops and some delicatessens.

Baked salmon with tabbouleh and tahini sauce

PESCATARIAN | PREP + COOK TIME **50 MINUTES** | SERVES **4**

Sumac adds a tart, lemony flavour to dishes making it a perfect pairing with fish. The Romans used this ground spice as a sour element in cooking before lemons were introduced to their culinary world. It also goes well with chicken and meat, sprinkled on vegetables, or in a salad dressing – any foods you would ordinarily match with a fresh citrus flavour.

700g piece skinless boneless salmon fillet

1½ tsp sumac

2 tbsp extra virgin olive oil

salt and freshly ground black pepper

lemon wedges, to serve

tabbouleh

1 cup (30g) small fresh flat-leaf parsley leaves

¼ cup (12g) small fresh mint leaves

2 green onions (spring onions), thinly sliced

½ cup (80g) coarse bulgur (bulgur wheat)

1½ cups (375ml) water

200g baby heirloom tomatoes, quartered (see tips)

1 tbsp lemon juice

tahini sauce

½ cup (140g) Greek yogurt

1½ tbsp tahini

1 garlic clove, crushed

2 tsp lemon juice

1 To make the tabbouleh, combine the herbs and green onion in a large bowl; reserve half the mixture for serving. Bring the bulgur and water to the boil in a small saucepan; reduce heat to low. Cook for 20 minutes or until tender; drain. Transfer the bulgur to a large bowl; add the tomato and lemon juice. Toss gently to combine; season with salt and pepper to taste.

2 To make the tahini sauce, whisk the ingredients in a small bowl until combined; season with salt and pepper to taste.

3 Preheat oven to 200°C/400°F.

4 Line an oven tray with baking paper. Place the salmon on the tray; sprinkle with 1 teaspoon of the sumac, then drizzle with the olive oil. Season with salt and pepper. Bake for 20 minutes or until the salmon is almost cooked through.

5 Top the baked salmon with the reserved herb mixture and remaining sumac; serve with the tabbouleh, tahini sauce, and lemon wedges.

TIPS

- Use regular cherry or plum tomatoes, if preferred.
- You can make the tabbouleh and tahini sauce several hours ahead; refrigerate, covered, until ready to use.

Almond gremolata roast chicken

PREP + COOK TIME **2 HOURS** | SERVES **4**

Gremolata is a versatile condiment and garnish – sprinkled on a dish just before serving, the scent of the combined ingredients once they hit the heat excites the palate. Originally based on garlic, lemon rind, and parsley, there are many variations using other citrus rinds, or pine nuts and finely grated parmesan. We've added roasted almonds for flavour and crunch.

$^1/_2$ cup (80g) roasted almonds, chopped

4 fresh sage leaves

1 tsp finely grated lemon rind (see tip)

2 garlic cloves, coarsely chopped

$^1/_3$ cup (80ml) extra virgin olive oil

salt and freshly ground black pepper

1.8kg whole chicken

$^1/_4$ bunch celery (375g), pale inner leaves reserved

$^1/_4$ loaf (150g) sourdough bread, torn into 4cm pieces

2 parsnips (240g), cut into eighths

2 bunches (800g) rainbow baby carrots, trimmed, halved lengthways

1 cup (250ml) chicken stock

almond gremolata

$^1/_2$ cup (80g) finely chopped roasted almonds

1 small garlic clove, crushed

3 tsp finely grated lemon rind (see tip)

$^1/_3$ cup finely chopped fresh flat-leaf parsley leaves

1 Preheat oven to 200°C (180°C fan/400°F/Gas 6). Oil a large roasting pan.

2 Blend or process the almonds, sage, lemon rind, garlic, and $1^1/_2$ tablespoons of olive oil until a rough paste forms; season with salt and pepper.

3 Pat the chicken dry with paper towel. Spread the almond mixture evenly between the chicken skin and breast and tops of the legs. Place the chicken in the oiled pan; season with salt and pepper.

4 Place the celery around the chicken; top with the bread. Drizzle with another $1^1/_2$ tablespoons of the olive oil.

5 Place the parsnip, carrot, and stock in another large roasting pan; drizzle with the remaining olive oil. Season with salt and pepper. Roast the chicken and vegetables for $1^1/_4$ hours or until the chicken is cooked through. Transfer the chicken, breast-side down, to a tray; cover loosely with foil. Stand for 15 minutes. Roast the vegetables for a further 20 minutes or until golden and tender.

6 Meanwhile, make the almond gremolata. Combine the ingredients in a small bowl; season with salt and pepper to taste.

7 Serve the chicken with the sourdough and vegetables, sprinkled with the almond gremolata.

TIP

Use orange rind instead of lemon rind in the chicken coating and gremolata, if you like.

Provençale beef casserole

PREP + COOK TIME **1 HOURS 50 MINUTES** | SERVES **4**

If you wouldn't drink it, don't cook with it: that's the rule of thumb for choosing wine for cooking. Cheap, inferior quality wines will impart a less pleasant flavour than a great drinking wine. Serve a hearty casserole such as this with mashed potato or crusty bread to mop up the sauce.

2 tbsp extra virgin olive oil

1kg stewing beef, cut into 2cm pieces (see tip)

2 rindless bacon slices (130g), coarsely chopped

1 medium leek (350g), thinly sliced

2 medium carrots (240g), diced

1 celery stalk (150g), trimmed, diced

2 garlic cloves, crushed

400g can chopped tomatoes

1½ cups (375ml) beef stock

1 cup (250ml) dry red wine

2 bay leaves

4 sprigs fresh thyme

6 sprigs fresh flat-leaf parsley

2 medium courgettes (240g), thickly sliced

½ cup (75g) pitted black olives

1 Heat the olive oil in large heavy-based saucepan; cook the beef, in batches, until browned. Remove from the pan.

2 Cook the bacon, leek, carrot, celery, and garlic in the same pan, stirring, for 5 minutes or until the leek softens.

3 Return the beef to the pan, add the tomatoes, stock, wine, bay leaves, thyme, and parsley; bring to the boil. Reduce heat to low; cook, covered, for 1 hour, stirring occasionally.

4 Add the courgettes and olives; cook, covered, for 30 minutes or until the beef is tender. Remove and discard the thyme and parsley before serving.

TIP

Stewing beef is a cut that comes from the shin area and cooks well in a shorter period of time. When the bone is left in it is also known as Osso Bucco which is used across Italian dishes.

Seeded carrot and cabbage filo pie

VEGETARIAN | PREP + COOK TIME **1 HOUR + COOLING** | SERVES **6**

Seeds and nuts are little nutritional powerhouses. Walnuts in particular offer an array of antioxidant and anti-inflammatory nutrients, as well as valuable monosaturated and omega-3 fatty acids. Roasting seeds and nuts amplifies their flavour and, if they're a little on the stale side, will freshen them up.

½ cup (125ml) extra virgin olive oil

1 large leek (500g), white part only, thinly sliced

3 garlic cloves, crushed

2 tsp caraway seeds

3 medium carrots (360g), coarsely grated

375g savoy cabbage, shredded

⅓ cup (55g) currants

⅓ cup (16g) finely chopped fresh mint

14 sheets filo pastry (210g)

seed topping

¼ cup (50g) pepitas (pumpkin seeds)

¼ cup (35g) slivered almonds

¼ cup (25g) coarsely chopped walnuts

1 tbsp poppy seeds

1 tbsp sesame seeds

herb salad

1 medium cucumber (130g)

½ cup (30g) fresh flat-leaf parsley leaves

½ cup (30g) fresh curly parsley leaves

¼ cup (12g) fresh mint leaves

¼ cup (6g) fresh dill

2 green onions (spring onions), thinly sliced

1 tbsp red wine vinegar

2 tbsp extra virgin olive oil

salt and freshly ground black pepper

1 Heat ⅓ cup (80ml) of the olive oil in a large frying pan over a medium heat; cook the leek, garlic, and caraway seeds for 5 minutes. Add the carrot; cook for 3 minutes. Add the cabbage; cook for a further 5 minutes or until the vegetables are soft. Stir in the currants and mint. Cool.

2 Make the seed topping. Combine the ingredients in a small bowl.

3 Preheat oven to 180°C (160°C fan/350°F/Gas 4).

4 Divide the filling into seven portions. Brush one sheet of pastry with a little of the olive oil; top with a second sheet. Keep the remaining sheets covered with baking paper topped with a clean, damp tea towel to prevent them from drying out. Place one portion of the filling lengthways, in a thin line, along the pastry edge; roll the pastry over the filling. Starting at the centre of a 24cm springform pan, carefully form the pastry roll, seam-side down, into a coil. Repeat with the remaining pastry sheets, olive oil, and filling, joining each roll to the end of the last one and coiling it around until the bottom of the pan is covered. Brush the top with olive oil.

5 Bake the filo pie for 20 minutes. Cover the pie evenly with the seed topping; bake for a further 10 minutes or until golden.

6 Meanwhile, make the herb salad. Using a vegetable peeler, peel the cucumber into ribbons. Place the cucumber in a medium bowl, add the remaining ingredients; toss gently to combine. Season with salt and pepper to taste.

7 Serve the filo pie with the herb salad.

Lamb bretonne

PREP + COOK TIME **2 HOURS 30 MINUTES** | SERVES **4**

Hearty and comforting, this French-style lamb roast will become a Sunday favourite. The lamb leg is prepared in the classic way, pierced all over, then studded with garlic and rosemary. For the French twist from Brittany, add white beans, tomatoes, and stock before putting it in the oven for 2 hours. Serve with mashed potatoes and steamed green vegetables.

1.5kg leg of lamb

1 garlic clove, thinly sliced

2 sprigs fresh rosemary

salt and freshly ground black pepper

1 tbsp extra virgin olive oil

2 medium onions (300g), thinly sliced

3 garlic cloves, crushed

400g can chopped tomatoes

410g tomato puree (passata)

2 cups (500ml) beef stock

400g can cannellini beans, drained, rinsed (see tip)

1 Preheat oven to 180°C (160°C fan/350°F/Gas 4).

2 Trim the excess fat from the lamb. Pierce the lamb in several places with a sharp knife; press the sliced garlic and a little of the rosemary firmly into the cuts. Season the lamb with salt and pepper.

3 Heat the olive oil in a large flameproof roasting pan over a medium heat; cook the onion and garlic, stirring, for 5 minutes or until the onion browns slightly. Stir in the tomatoes, puree, stock, beans, and remaining rosemary; bring to the boil.

4 Place the lamb, pierced-side down, on the bean mixture, cover; transfer to the oven. Cook for 1 hour. Uncover, turn the lamb carefully; cook, brushing occasionally with the tomato mixture, for 1 hour for medium or until the lamb is cooked as desired.

TIP

Use canned borlotti beans instead of cannellini beans, if you like.

Black rice seafood paella

PESCATARIAN | PREP + COOK TIME **1 HOUR** | SERVES **6**

Short-grain rice varieties such as black rice are the most suitable for paella. It adds a lovely nutty taste and becomes almost purple in colour when cooked. The traditional pan for this Spanish recipe is shallow and wide. If you don't have a paella pan or heavy-based frying pan large enough, use two smaller frying pans as the mixture should only be about 4cm deep.

8 uncooked large king prawns (560g)

¼ cup (60ml) extra virgin olive oil

1 medium white onion (150g), finely chopped

1½ tsp smoked paprika

1 small red capsicum (pepper) (150g), thickly sliced

2 garlic cloves, chopped

1 cup (200g) black rice, rinsed

400g can cherry tomatoes

2 cups (500ml) vegetable stock

2 cups (500ml) water

300g skinless boneless firm white fish fillets, cut into 4cm pieces

4 scallops on half shell (100g)

8 pipis (clams) (320g)

salt and freshly ground black pepper

¼ cup (15g) fresh flat-leaf parsley leaves

lemon wedges, to serve

1 Shell and devein the prawns, leaving the tails intact.

2 Heat the olive oil in a large heavy-based frying pan or paella pan over a medium heat; cook the onion, stirring, for 3 minutes or until softened. Add the paprika, capsicum, garlic, and rice; cook, stirring, for 2 minutes or until well combined. Add the tomatoes, stock, and water; bring to the boil. Reduce heat to low; cook, stirring occasionally, for 40 minutes or until most of the liquid has been absorbed and the rice is tender.

3 Arrange the seafood on the rice mixture; season with salt and pepper. Cook, covered, for 5 minutes or until the seafood is just cooked through.

4 Serve the paella with parsley and lemon wedges.

TIP

Black rice is available from some supermarkets and Asian food stores.

SALADS
AND SIDES

From colourful salads packed with flavour
and vibrancy to grains, fish, and delicious
dips, these dishes are good enough to
take centre stage.

Pumpkin fatteh with almond skordalia

VEGAN | PREP + COOK TIME **45 MINUTES** | SERVES **4**

Fatteh is an Arabic word meaning "crushed" or "crumbs". In a recipe it refers to fresh or toasted flatbreads covered with other ingredients, such as the vegetables in this salad. You could make extra and use as an accompaniment to dip or salsa, or as a healthy snack, or serve as a starter for a shared meal.

800g small kent pumpkin, cut into thin wedges (see tips)

$1/4$ cup (60ml) extra virgin olive oil

$1^1/2$ tbsp za'atar

salt and freshly ground black pepper

2 medium red capsicums (peppers) (400g), thickly sliced

1 medium red onion (170g), thickly sliced

1 large wholemeal Lebanese bread round (100g), split into two rounds

300g canned chickpeas, drained, rinsed

2 tbsp pine nuts, toasted

$1/3$ cup (15g) fresh flat-leaf parsley leaves

$1/3$ cup (16g) fresh mint leaves

lemon wedges, to serve

almond skordalia

1 cup (160g) blanched almonds

2 garlic cloves, crushed

1 cup (70g) coarsely chopped day-old bread

2 tbsp white wine vinegar

$1/3$ cup (80ml) extra virgin olive oil

$1/2$ cup (125ml) water

1   Preheat oven 220°C (200°C fan/425°F/Gas 7). Line two large oven trays with baking paper.

2   Place the pumpkin wedges on one tray; drizzle with 1 tablespoon of the olive oil and sprinkle with 1 tablespoon of the za'atar; season with salt and pepper. Roast for 30 minutes or until just tender. Meanwhile, place the capsicum and onion on the second tray; drizzle with another tablespoon of the olive oil. Season with salt and pepper; roast for 20 minutes or until tender.

3   Place the bread on a third unlined oven tray, lightly brush with the remaining olive oil; season with salt and pepper. Toast the bread for 3 minutes or until crisp; cool. Break into pieces.

4   Make the almond skordalia. Place the almonds in a heavy-based frying pan; stir constantly over a medium to high heat until they are browned evenly. Remove from the pan; cool. Process the almonds, garlic, bread, and vinegar until wet breadcrumbs form. With the motor operating, gradually add the olive oil in a thin, steady stream; add the water, process until the mixture is smooth. Season with salt and pepper to taste.

5   Place the vegetables, chickpeas, pine nuts, parsley, and mint on a platter; top with the remaining za'atar. Serve with the almond skordalia, toasted bread, and lemon wedges.

TIPS

- You could use the more readily available butternut pumpkin (butternut squash) instead of kent pumpkin.
- You can assemble the salad ahead of time, omitting the bread. Serve bread on the salad, or on the side.

Baby beetroot, lentil, and watercress salad

VEGAN | PREP + COOK TIME **40 MINUTES** | SERVES **4**

French-style green lentils are closely related to the famous French lentils du puy; these green-blue, tiny lentils have a nutty, earthy flavour and a hardy nature that allows them to be rapidly cooked without disintegrating. Because they hold their shape better than ordinary lentils, they are perfect for a hearty salad, and make a great addition to soups and stews.

1kg baby beetroot, stems and leaves attached

2 garlic cloves, sliced

¼ cup (15g) fresh rosemary leaves

2 tbsp extra virgin olive oil

¼ cup (60ml) balsamic vinegar

½ cup (100g) dried French-style green lentils, rinsed

3 cups (90g) trimmed watercress

1 large pomegranate (430g), seeds removed (see tip)

⅓ cup (45g) roasted hazelnuts, halved

salt and freshly ground black pepper

1 Preheat oven to 200°C (180°C fan/400°F/Gas 6).

2 Trim the beetroot tops to 4cm; reserve a few small leaves. Halve the beetroot, or quarter if large. Place the beetroot, garlic, and rosemary in a large ovenproof dish; drizzle with the olive oil and vinegar. Roast for 30 minutes or until tender.

3 Meanwhile, place the lentils in a medium saucepan; cover with water. Bring to the boil; cook the lentils for 25 minutes or until tender. Drain; rinse under cold water, drain.

4 Place the lentils, roast beetroot and cooking juices, watercress, half the pomegranate seeds, and half the hazelnuts in a large bowl; toss gently to combine. Season with salt and pepper to taste.

5 Transfer to a large bowl or platter; top with the remaining pomegranate seeds and hazelnuts, and the reserved beetroot leaves.

TIP

To remove the seeds from the pomegranate, cut in half crossways; hold a half, cut-side down, in the palm of your hand over a small bowl, then hit the outside firmly with a wooden spoon. The seeds should fall out easily; discard any white pith that falls out with them. Repeat with the other half.

Roasted carrot, radish, and egg salad with romesco sauce

VEGETARIAN | PREP + COOK TIME **40 MINUTES** | SERVES **4**

Originating in the Catalonia area of Spain, romesco is a sauce consisting of blended almonds and red capsicum. During the springtime, romesco is served as a dip for calçots, a spring onion native to Catalonia, which are roasted over an open fire until charred. It is a great dairy-free alternative to creamy sauces and pesto.

800g rainbow baby carrots, trimmed

1¹/₂ tbsp extra virgin olive oil

salt and freshly ground black pepper

4 eggs

300g small radishes, trimmed, halved

¹/₃ cup (15g) fresh flat-leaf parsley leaves

romesco sauce

260g jar roasted red capsicums (peppers), drained

1 garlic clove, crushed

¹/₂ cup (80g) blanched almonds, roasted

2 tbsp sherry vinegar

1 tsp smoked paprika

2 tbsp chopped fresh flat-leaf parsley leaves

¹/₃ cup (80ml) extra virgin olive oil

1 Preheat oven to 200°C (180°C fan/400°F/Gas 6).

2 Place carrots on a large oven tray, drizzle with olive oil; season with salt. Roast for 20 minutes or until tender and lightly browned.

3 Meanwhile, make the romesco sauce. Process the ingredients until smooth; season with salt and pepper to taste.

4 Place the eggs in a small saucepan, cover with cold water; bring to the boil. Cook for 2 minutes or until soft-boiled; drain. Rinse under cold water; drain. When cool enough to handle, peel the eggs; tear in half.

5 Place the carrots, radish, and eggs on a platter. Top with parsley; season with pepper. Serve with the romesco sauce.

TIP

Traditionally used to accompany fish, you could also pair the romesco sauce with lamb or chicken, or serve with crudités and crisp breads as a tasty dip.

Roasted cauliflower, cavolo nero, and spiced chickpeas

VEGAN | PREP + COOK TIME **40 MINUTES** | SERVES **4**

Chickpeas are an often overlooked legume, full of protein, fibre, and folate. They are one of the oldest cultivated legumes in the world with 7,500-year-old remains found in the Middle East. Chickpeas can be cooked and eaten cold in salads, ground into flour, fried as falafel, baked into a flatbread, used in stews, or blended to make hummus.

1 small cauliflower (1kg), trimmed, cut into small florets

220g brussels sprouts, trimmed, sliced

2 tbsp extra virgin olive oil

salt and freshly ground black pepper

400g can chickpeas, drained, rinsed

1 tsp smoked paprika

1 tsp ground cumin

1 tsp ground coriander

12 cavolo nero leaves (120g), trimmed, torn

1 fresh long red chilli, seeded, chopped finely

tahini dressing

1 tbsp tahini

1 tbsp pomegranate molasses (see tips)

1 small garlic clove, crushed

$1/4$ cup (60ml) water

1 Preheat oven to 200°C (180°C fan/400°F/Gas 6).

2 Place the cauliflower and brussels sprouts on an oven tray; drizzle with half the olive oil. Season with salt and pepper; toss to coat in the oil. Place the chickpeas on another oven tray; sprinkle with the paprika, cumin, and coriander. Season with salt and pepper; drizzle with the remaining oil.

3 Roast the vegetables and chickpeas for 25 minutes. Add the cavolo nero to the vegetables; roast for a further 5 minutes or until the vegetables are tender and the chickpeas are crisp.

4 Meanwhile, make the tahini dressing. Combine the ingredients in a small bowl; season with salt and pepper to taste.

5 Drizzle the vegetables and chickpeas with the dressing and sprinkle with the chilli; serve.

TIPS

- Pomegranate molasses is available from Middle Eastern food stores, major supermarkets, specialty food shops, and some delicatessens.
- This salad is best served either warm or at room temperature.

Chermoula tuna, chickpea, and broad bean salad

PESCATARIAN | PREP + COOK TIME **30 MINUTES + REFRIGERATION** | SERVES **2**

Chermoula is a spice marinade that contains the core ingredients of garlic, cumin, coriander, oil, and salt. Traditionally used to flavour fish or seafood, you could make double the recipe and use it to dress other meats and vegetables, adding a fresh element to simple dishes. If the chermoula ingredients aren't blending well, add 1 tablespoon of water to the mixture.

300g piece tuna steak (see tips)

1 cup (150g) frozen broad beans

150g green beans, trimmed, halved lengthways

400g can chickpeas, drained, rinsed

1/2 cup (30g) fresh flat-leaf parsley leaves

1 medium lemon (140g), segmented (see tips)

1 tbsp lemon juice

1 tbsp extra virgin olive oil

chermoula

1/2 small red onion (50g), coarsely chopped

1 garlic clove, peeled

1 cup (16g) fresh coriander leaves, coarsely chopped

1 cup (60g) fresh flat-leaf parsley leaves, coarsely chopped

1 tsp ground cumin

1 tsp smoked paprika

1 tbsp extra virgin olive oil

salt and freshly ground black pepper

1 Make the chermoula. Blend or process the ingredients until just combined; season with salt and pepper to taste. Reserve three-quarters of the chermoula to serve.

2 Place the tuna in a shallow dish with the remaining chermoula; toss to coat. Cover; refrigerate for 30 minutes.

3 Meanwhile, cook the broad beans and green beans in a large saucepan of boiling water for 2 minutes or until just tender; drain. Refresh under cold running water; drain well. Separate the broad beans; remove grey skins from the broad beans.

4 Cook the tuna on a heated oiled grill plate or barbecue over a medium heat for 2 minutes each side or until slightly charred on the outside but still rare in the centre; cover loosely with foil, stand for 5 minutes. Cut the tuna, across the grain, into slices.

5 Combine the broad beans, green beans, chickpeas, parsley, and lemon segments in a medium bowl with the combined lemon juice and olive oil. Serve the tuna and salad topped with the reserved chermoula.

TIPS

• Purchase sashimi-grade tuna for this recipe. Alternatively, swap the tuna for salmon, if you like.

• To segment a lemon, use a small sharp knife to cut the top and bottom from the lemon. Cut off the rind with the white pith, following the curve of the fruit. Holding the lemon over a bowl, cut down both sides of the white membrane to release each segment.

Mountain rice salad with haloumi

VEGETARIAN | PREP + COOK TIME **50 MINUTES** | SERVES **4**

Haloumi is a Cypriot semi-hard, unripened brined cheese, often made from a mixture of goat's and sheep's milk. Its high melting point allows for it to hold its shape while being either fried or grilled. You shouldn't allow haloumi to become cold after it is cooked, as it becomes chewy and not nearly as delectable as when soft and golden straight from the grill.

¼ cup (60ml) red wine vinegar

1 tbsp Dijon mustard

¼ cup (60ml) extra virgin olive oil

¼ cup (90g) honey

1 cup (200g) mountain rice blend (see tips)

500g frozen broad beans

1 baby fennel bulb (130g), trimmed, thinly sliced

100g radishes, thinly sliced

¼ cup (7g) coarsely chopped fresh dill

250g haloumi, cut into 1cm slices

1 Place the red wine vinegar, mustard, 2 tablespoons of olive oil, and 2 tablespoons of honey in a screw-top jar; shake well. Season with salt and pepper to taste.

2 Cook the rice in a large saucepan of boiling water for 20 minutes or until tender; drain. Rinse under cold water; drain well.

3 Cook the broad beans in a large saucepan of boiling water for 2 minutes or until just tender; drain. Refresh under cold running water, drain well; remove grey skins.

4 Place the rice in a large bowl with half the dressing; mix well. Add the broad beans, fennel, radishes, and dill; toss gently to combine.

5 Heat the remaining oil in a large non-stick frying pan over a medium-high heat; cook the haloumi for 1 minute on each side or until golden brown. Drizzle with the remaining honey.

6 Place the rice salad on a large platter; top with the haloumi and pan juices. Just before serving, drizzle with the remaining dressing.

TIPS

- Mountain rice blend is a combination of equal parts brown rice, black rice, and red rice.
- You can use frozen peas instead of broad beans, if preferred.
- Sprinkle with dill sprigs before serving, if you like.

Salad niçoise

PESCATARIAN | PREP + COOK TIME **45 MINUTES** | SERVES **4**

Referred to as "one of the best combinations of salad ingredients ever invented", this salad is named after its place of origin, the French city of Nice. Popularized by celebrity chefs, salad niçoise is now found all over the world, and like all great dishes, is the centre of great debate as to what should or should not go into it.

600g baby new potatoes, halved

200g green beans, trimmed, halved

3 eggs

2 x 200g thick-cut tuna steaks (see tips)

1 tbsp extra virgin olive oil

salt and freshly ground black pepper

1/2 small red onion (50g), thinly sliced

250g cherry tomatoes, halved

1/3 cup (40g) pitted small black olives

1/3 cup (55g) caperberries, rinsed (see tips)

1/4 cup (5g) small fresh basil leaves

2 tbsp coarsely chopped fresh flat-leaf parsley leaves

dressing

2 tbsp extra virgin olive oil

2 tbsp white wine vinegar

2 tsp lemon juice

1 Place the potatoes in a small saucepan, cover with cold water; bring to the boil. Cook for 15 minutes or until tender; drain.

2 Meanwhile, boil, steam, or microwave the beans until tender; drain. Refresh under cold running water; drain well.

3 To make the dressing, place the ingredients in a small screw-top jar; shake well. Season with salt and pepper to taste.

4 Place the hot potatoes in a large bowl with one-third of the dressing; toss gently to combine.

5 Place the eggs in a small saucepan, cover with cold water; bring to the boil. Cook for 2 minutes or until soft-boiled; drain. Rinse under cold water; drain. When the eggs are cool enough to handle, peel; tear in half.

6 Brush the tuna with olive oil; season with salt and pepper. Heat a large heavy-based frying pan over a high heat; cook the tuna for 1 minute on each side for medium-rare or until cooked as desired. Cut into thin slices.

7 Add the beans, onion, tomatoes, eggs, olives, caperberries, herbs, and the remaining dressing to the bowl; toss gently to combine. Serve topped with the tuna.

TIPS

- Use canned tuna in oil instead of fresh tuna, if you like.
- Omit the caperberries, if you prefer.

Barbecued octopus

PESCATARIAN | PREP + COOK TIME **30 MINUTES + REFRIGERATION** | SERVES **4**

Octopus is usually tenderized before you buy it. Like squid, octopus requires either long slow cooking (usually for larger molluscs) or quick cooking over a high heat (usually for small molluscs) – anything in between will make them tough and rubbery. When barbecuing, make sure the grill plate or barbecue is very hot before adding the baby octopus.

3 medium lemons (420g)

⅓ cup (80ml) extra virgin olive oil

½ tsp dried oregano leaves

2 garlic cloves, crushed

salt and freshly ground black pepper

1kg baby octopus, cleaned (see tips)

4 fresh long red chillies

rocket leaves, to serve

fresh flat-leaf parsley leaves, to serve

1 Finely grate the rind from 1 lemon; squeeze out the juice. Place the rind, juice, olive oil, oregano, and garlic in a screw-top jar; shake well. Season with salt and pepper to taste.

2 Place the octopus and half the dressing in a large bowl; toss to coat in the mixture. Cover; refrigerate for 30 minutes.

3 Cook the octopus on a heated grill plate (or pan or barbecue) over a high heat for 6 minutes or until browned and tender. Cover loosely with foil.

4 Cut the remaining lemons in half crossways; cook, cut-side down, on a heated grill plate (or pan or barbecue) for 2 minutes or until browned. Transfer to a plate. Cook the whole chillies for 4 minutes or until slightly blackened; slice thickly.

5 Combine the octopus with the remaining dressing, chilli, and leaves; serve with the char-grilled lemons.

TIPS

- Ask your fishmonger to clean the octopus for you.
- Preheat the grill plate for at least 10 minutes before cooking for really fast, high-heat cooking.
- If you have nasturtium leaves, sprinkle these over the salad as well, if you like.

Delicious dips

Dips are great to serve at a party or as part of a mezze banquet. They're a commununal affair as guests gather around and share in the delicious offerings. These Mediterranean dips work well with raw vegetables, pitta bread, or served as accompaniments to a main meal.

Tzatziki

VEGETARIAN | PREP + COOK TIME **15 MINUTES + REFRIGERATION**
MAKES **1³/₄ CUPS**

Place a fine sieve over a bowl, spoon in 500g Greek yogurt and ¹/₂ teaspoon of salt. Cover, refrigerate for 2 hours or until thickened; discard liquid. Meanwhile, combine 1 coarsely grated medium cucumber and ¹/₂ teaspoon of salt in a small bowl; stand for 20 minutes. Squeeze out excess liquid from the cucumber. Combine the yogurt, cucumber, 1 crushed garlic clove, and 2 tablespoons of chopped fresh mint leaves; season with salt and pepper to taste.

Taramasalata

PESCATARIAN | PREP TIME **25 MINUTES + REFRIGERATION**
MAKES **1²/₃ CUPS**

Boil, steam, or microwave 1 coarsely chopped large potato until tender; cool. Refrigerate until cold. Mash the potato in a small bowl with 90g tarama (salted fish roe), ¹/₂ finely grated small white onion, ³/₄ cup extra virgin olive oil, ¹/₄ cup white wine vinegar, and 1 tablespoon of lemon juice until smooth. Season with pepper; serve drizzled with extra olive oil.

Butter bean hummus

VEGETARIAN | PREP + COOK TIME **10 MINUTES** | MAKES **3 CUPS**

Drain and rinse 2 x 400g cans butter beans. Blend or process the beans with ¹/₂ cup warm water, ¹/₄ cup tahini, ¹/₄ cup Greek yogurt, 2 tablespoons of lemon juice, 2 crushed garlic cloves, and 3 teaspoons of ground cumin until smooth; season with salt and pepper to taste. Sprinkle with ground cumin to serve.

CLOCKWISE from top

Beetroot, haloumi, chickpea, and rice salad

VEGETARIAN | PREP + COOK TIME **30 MINUTES** | SERVES **4**

Canned chickpeas must be drained of their liquid before using. Empty the contents of the can
into a strainer, allowing the liquid to drain away. Hold the strainer under cold running water
and rinse the chickpeas. The chickpea liquid, called aquafaba, can be reserved and whipped
into peaks like you would egg white, for a vegan-friendly meringue, pavlova, or mousse.

1 cup (200g) brown rice

1/3 cup (80ml) extra virgin olive oil

1 small red onion (100g), cut into wedges

1 tsp ground cumin

1 tsp ground coriander

400g can chickpeas, drained, rinsed

500g packaged pre-cooked beetroot, quartered

100g baby spinach leaves

1 cup (50g) fresh mint leaves

1/2 cup (50g) walnuts, roasted, coarsely chopped

2 tbsp balsamic glaze

salt and freshly ground black pepper

200g haloumi, sliced (see tip)

1 Cook the rice in a large saucepan of boiling water for 25 minutes or until just tender; drain.

2 Meanwhile, heat 1 tablespoon of olive oil in a large frying pan over a medium heat. Add the onion; cook, stirring, for 5 minutes or until tender. Add the cumin and coriander; cook, stirring, for 30 seconds or until fragrant. Add the chickpeas and beetroot; stir until heated through.

3 Meanwhile, combine the rice, spinach, mint, and walnuts in a large bowl. Drizzle with combined 1 tablespoon of balsamic glaze and 2 tablespoons of olive oil. Add the beetroot and chickpea mixture; toss gently. Season with salt and pepper.

4 Heat the remaining olive oil in a large frying pan over a high heat. Cook the haloumi for 2 minutes on each side or until golden.

5 Serve the salad with the haloumi, drizzled with the remaining balsamic glaze.

TIP

You can replace the haloumi with crumbled
goat's cheese or feta, if you like.

Green barley salad

VEGETARIAN | PREP + COOK TIME **30 MINUTES** | SERVES **6**

When in season, buy fresh broad beans in the pod for this recipe; you will need to remove the outer shell. Once the broad beans are blanched, pop the bright green beans from their leathery grey overcoats while they are still warm. Blanching peas and beans briefly helps to retain their bright spring colour.

1 cup (200g) pearl barley

3 cups (750ml) water

1 cup (120g) frozen peas

1 cup (150g) frozen broad beans (see tips)

150g green beans, trimmed, halved lengthways

1 medium cucumber (130g), halved lengthways, thinly sliced

1 baby cos lettuce (180g), trimmed, torn

2 green onions (spring onions), thinly sliced

1/2 cup (25g) fresh mint leaves

2 tbsp extra virgin olive oil

1 tbsp lemon juice

335g labneh in olive oil, drained (see tips)

salt and freshly ground black pepper

1 Place the pearl barley and water in a medium saucepan, bring to the boil; reduce heat to low. Cook, covered, for 35 minutes or until tender. Drain; rinse under cold water until cool.

2 Meanwhile, cook the peas, broad beans, and green beans in a large saucepan of boiling water for 2 minutes or until just tender; drain. Refresh under cold running water; drain well. Remove the grey skins from the broad beans.

3 Transfer the barley and pea mixture to a large bowl; add the cucumber, lettuce, green onion, and mint. Drizzle with combined olive oil and lemon juice; toss gently to combine.

4 Top the salad with labneh and season with salt and pepper to taste.

TIPS

- If fresh broad beans in the pod are available, use 500g of these instead to yield 1 cup (150g) of podded beans.
- Use your favourite feta instead of labneh, if you like.

Mediterranean grain salad with honey-cumin labneh

VEGETARIAN | PREP + COOK TIME **45 MINUTES** | SERVES **6**

Wholegrains, such as the brown rice and quinoa in this recipe, are great plant sources of protein and fibre, as well as a host of vitamins, minerals, and phytochemicals that improve your health. Seeds and nuts are also packed with vitamins and minerals, as well as omega-3 fats.

$^3/_4$ cup (150g) brown rice

$^1/_2$ cup (100g) French-style green lentils, rinsed

$^1/_2$ cup (100g) red quinoa

1 cup (250ml) water

1 small red onion (100g), finely chopped

2 tbsp pepitas (pumpkin seeds), toasted (see tip)

2 tbsp sunflower seeds, toasted (see tip)

2 tbsp pine nuts, toasted (see tip)

2 tbsp capers

$^1/_2$ cup (80g) currants

1 cup (60g) fresh flat-leaf parsley leaves

1 cup (16g) fresh coriander leaves

$^1/_4$ cup (60ml) lemon juice

$^1/_3$ cup (80ml) extra virgin olive oil

1 tsp cumin seeds, toasted (see tip)

1 cup (280g) labneh

1$^1/_2$ tbsp honey

$^1/_2$ cup (40g) flaked almonds, toasted (see tip)

1 Preheat the oven to 180°C (160°C fan/350°F/Gas 4). Place the seeds, pine nuts, and sliced almonds on a baking sheet, putting the cumin seeds and sliced almonds on small pieces of foil to keep them separate. Toast them for 8 minutes, stirring halfway through cooking time.

2 Meanwhile, cook the rice and lentils in separate large saucepans of boiling water for 25 minutes or until tender; drain, rinse well.

3 Place the quinoa in a small saucepan with the water, bring to the boil. Reduce heat to low; cook, covered, for 10 minutes or until tender. Drain.

4 Combine the cumin seeds and labneh in a small bowl; drizzle with honey.

5 Place the rice, lentils, and quinoa in a large bowl. Add the onion, seeds, pine nuts, capers, currants, herbs, lemon juice, and olive oil; stir until well combined.

6 Divide the salad among six plates; top with spoonfuls of the labneh mixture. Sprinkle with almonds.

Spicy pumpkin and cauliflower with rice and yogurt dressing

VEGETARIAN | PREP + COOK TIME **45 MINUTES** | SERVES **4**

Greek yogurt is a type of yogurt that has been strained to remove its whey (the liquid that remains in the cheese-making process), with a more sour taste and creamier texture than its commercial counterpart. Rich in calcium, good fats, and probiotics, which are essential for good gut health, Greek yogurt is a great addition to your diet.

750g kent pumpkin, cut into thin wedges (see tips)

750g cauliflower, cut into florets

2½ tbsp extra virgin olive oil

2 tsp ground coriander

2 tsp ground cumin

½ tsp ground cinnamon

salt and freshly ground back pepper

½ cup (100g) brown rice

8 cups (2 litres) water

2 tsp lemon juice

1 tbsp pepitas (pumpkin seeds)

1 tsp finely grated lemon rind

yogurt dressing

1 cup (280g) Greek yogurt

2 tbsp coarsely chopped fresh coriander

1 tsp finely grated lemon rind

1 tbsp lemon juice

1   Preheat oven to 200°C (180°C fan/400°F/Gas 6).

2   Combine the pumpkin, cauliflower, 1 tablespoon of the olive oil, and the spices on a large oven tray until the vegetables are well coated; spread evenly in a single layer. Season with salt and pepper. Roast for 30 minutes or until the vegetables are tender.

3   Meanwhile, place the rice and water in a medium saucepan; bring to the boil. Boil for 25 minutes or until the rice is tender. Drain well; transfer to a bowl. Add the remaining olive oil and the lemon juice; stir to combine.

4   Make the yogurt dressing. Combine the ingredients in a medium bowl; season with salt and pepper to taste.

5   Spoon the rice onto a large platter or among four plates; top evenly with the roasted vegetables. Spoon over a little of the dressing, sprinkle with the pepitas and lemon rind; serve with the remaining dressing.

TIPS

• Use the more readily available butternut pumpkin (butternut squash) instead of kent pumpkin, if preferred.

• Sprinkle with micro herbs before serving, if you like.

Barbecued calamari fattoush salad

PESCATARIAN | PREP + COOK TIME **50 MINUTES + REFRIGERATION** | SERVES **4**

Created as a way of using day-old pita, a Lebanese fattoush salad gives new life to stale bread by frying it until crisp and combining it with fresh vegetables for texture and taste. Calamari is eaten all across the Mediterranean region. Grilled, deep fried, or stuffed, it gives flavour and colour to Spanish and Italian dishes such as paella, risotto, soups, and pasta.

1½ tsp cumin seeds

1 tsp ground coriander

2 garlic cloves, crushed

½ tsp dried chilli flakes

¼ cup (60ml) extra virgin olive oil

2 tbsp lemon juice

6 medium calamari (720g), cleaned (see tips)

3 medium tomatoes (450g), coarsely chopped

1½ tsp sea salt flakes

1 medium cucumber (130g), halved lengthways, seeded, thinly sliced

1 cup (50g) fresh mint leaves

1 cup (60g) fresh flat-leaf parsley leaves

2 small wholemeal pocket pita breads (160g), split in half (see tips)

1 Heat a small frying pan over a medium heat. Cook the cumin seeds and coriander, stirring, for 2 minutes or until toasted and fragrant. Transfer to a medium bowl, add the garlic, chilli, olive oil, and lemon juice; stir to combine. Reserve 2 tablespoons of the spice mixture in a small bowl.

2 Using a sharp knife, cut the calamari hoods in half lengthways. Score the inside surface of the calamari in a criss-cross pattern at 1cm intervals. Cut into 4cm strips. Add the calamari hoods and tentacles to the spice mixture in the bowl; toss to coat. Refrigerate the calamari for 2 hours.

3 Meanwhile, combine the tomato and salt in a colander; stand it in the sink for 10 minutes to drain. Place the tomato, cucumber, mint, and parsley in a medium bowl; toss to combine.

4 Cook the pita and calamari hoods and tentacles on a heated oiled grill plate (or pan or barbecue) until the pita are toasted and the calamari is just cooked through.

5 Break the pita into bite-sized pieces. Add the reserved spice mixture and half the pita to the tomato mixture; toss to combine. Serve the calamari with the salad and remaining pita.

TIPS

- You could use cleaned squid hoods instead.
- If you are having difficulty splitting the pita breads open, microwave on HIGH (100%) for 10 seconds. The steam from heating in the microwave usually makes it easier to open the bread.

Chicken, bulgur, and pomegranate salad

PREP + COOK TIME **45 MINUTES + REFRIGERATION AND STANDING** | SERVES **6**

Since ancient times, pomegranates have been cultivated in the Mediterranean; its bright red arils, the seeds of the fruit, feature heavily in the art, poetry, and myths of the region, as well as in the cuisine.

¹/₄ cup (60ml) extra virgin olive oil

¹/₄ cup (60ml) pomegranate molasses (see tip)

1 tbsp ground cumin

2 garlic cloves, crushed

1kg chicken breast fillets

1¹/₂ cups (375ml) chicken stock

1¹/₂ cups (240g) fine bulgur (bulgur wheat)

1 small cauliflower (1kg)

salt and freshly ground black pepper

1 large pomegranate (430g), seeds removed

1 medium red onion (170g), halved, thinly sliced

1 cup (60g) fresh flat-leaf parsley leaves

1 cup (110g) coarsely chopped walnuts, roasted

150g Greek feta, crumbled

pomegranate dressing

¹/₄ cup (60ml) extra virgin olive oil

¹/₄ cup (60ml) lemon juice

3 tsp honey

3 tsp pomegranate molasses

1 Combine half the olive oil, the molasses, cumin, and garlic in a large bowl; add the chicken and turn to coat. Cover; refrigerate for 3 hours or overnight.

2 Bring the stock to the boil in a medium saucepan. Remove from the heat, add the bulgur; cover, stand for 5 minutes.

3 Meanwhile, preheat the grill. Trim the cauliflower; cut into 1.5cm florets. Place on an oven tray; drizzle with the remaining olive oil, season with salt and pepper. Grill the cauliflower for 8 minutes, turning halfway through cooking time, or until tender.

4 Make the pomegranate dressing. Place the ingredients in a screw-top jar; shake well. Season with salt and pepper to taste.

5 Drain the chicken; discard the marinade. Cook the chicken on a heated oiled grill plate (or pan or barbecue) for 4 minutes on each side or until cooked through. Stand, covered loosely with foil, for 10 minutes. Slice thickly.

6 Spoon the bulgur onto a platter or bowl; top with the chicken, cauliflower, and remaining ingredients. Drizzle with the dressing.

TIP

Pomegranate molasses is available from delis, Middle Eastern food stores, specialty food shops, and most major supermarkets.

DESSERTS

Round off your meal with the sweet flavours
of the Mediterranean – figs, honey, fruit
compotes, cakes, and baklava all feature in
this mouthwatering collection of desserts.

Spiced couscous with passionfruit yogurt

PREP + COOK TIME **25 MINUTES** | SERVES **4**

Couscous consists of steamed balls of crushed durum wheat semolina, with a similar nutritional value to pasta (although pasta is more refined). Originally a North African dish, it travelled to the Mediterranean in the 17th century, and is now widely eaten in the region. It is particularly popular in France, but is also common in Spain, Portugal, Italy, and Greece.

1 cup (200g) wholemeal couscous

2 tsp extra virgin olive oil

1 tsp mixed spice

1/4 tsp allspice

1/4 cup (90g) honey

1 cup (250ml) boiling water

1/2 cup (50g) walnuts, roasted

3/4 cup (200g) Greek yogurt

2 tbsp fresh passionfruit pulp

2 medium oranges (480g)

1/3 cup (50g) blueberries

2 tbsp fresh mint leaves

1 Combine the couscous, olive oil, mixed spice, allspice, a pinch of salt, and the honey with the boiling water in a medium bowl. Stand, covered, for 5 minutes or until all the liquid is absorbed. Fluff with a fork. Stir in the walnuts.

2 Meanwhile, combine the yogurt and passionfruit in a small bowl.

3 Finely grate the rind from one orange; you will need 1 teaspoon. Peel the oranges, then thinly slice. Serve the spiced couscous topped with the orange slices, blueberries, passionfruit yogurt, mint, and orange rind.

TIP

Swap the blueberries for strawberries or raspberries, or use a mixture of all three, if you like.

Honey and cherry barley pudding

PREP + COOK TIME **50 MINUTES** | SERVES **2**

One of the first cultivated grains in history, barley is a wonderfully versatile wholegrain, with
a rich nutty flavour, packed with fibre. Here we have used it to make a sweet pudding, but it
can also be used to bulk out a vegetable soup or in place of red meat in a hearty, winter stew.
Sheeps' milk yogurt can be purchased from health food stores and some supermarkets.

$^1/_2$ cup (100g) pearl barley (see tips)

1$^1/_2$ cups (375ml) water

1 cup (280g) sheep's milk yogurt

$^1/_2$ tsp ground cinnamon

1$^1/_2$ cups (185g) frozen pitted cherries, thawed,
halved (see tips)

30g fresh honeycomb, sliced

2 tbsp coarsely chopped natural almonds

ground cinnamon, extra, to serve

1   Place the pearl barley and water in a small saucepan, bring to the boil.
Reduce heat to low; cook, covered, for 35 minutes or until tender. Drain.
Rinse under cold water until cool; drain well.

2   Combine the pearl barley, yogurt, cinnamon, and $^2/_3$ cup of cherries
in a medium bowl. Divide between two bowls. Top with the remaining
cherries, the honeycomb, and the almonds; dust with the extra
ground cinnamon.

TIPS

- You could also try this with cooked quinoa instead
of pearl barley.
- Frozen raspberries can be used instead of cherries.
- Use fresh pitted cherries when in season.

Sweet fig bruschetta

PREP + COOK TIME **10 MINUTES** | SERVES **4**

Figs are one of the most recognizable Mediterranean fruits, featuring heavily in the art and myths of the region. In fact, figs are thought to be the first fruit to be cultivated by humans for food, and were widely consumed in ancient Greece and Rome. Try to use local honey for this recipe, rather than commercial honey that has been highly refined.

6 medium figs (360g), halved

1/3 cup (115g) honey

2 tbsp cold water

2/3 cup (190g) Greek yogurt

1/3 cup (85g) mascarpone

1 tbsp icing sugar

4 thick slices sourdough bread (280g), toasted

2 tbsp coarsely chopped walnuts (see tip)

1 Heat a large non-stick frying pan over a medium-high heat. Drizzle the cut-sides of the figs with honey. Cook the figs, cut-side down, for 2 minutes or until glazed and warmed through. Add the water to the pan; remove from heat.

2 Meanwhile, whisk the yogurt, mascarpone, and sifted icing sugar in a small bowl until combined.

3 Spread the toast evenly with the mascarpone mixture; top with the figs and walnuts. Before serving, drizzle with the cooking juices.

TIP

You can use chopped pistachios or flaked almonds instead of walnuts, if you like.

Whole orange semolina cake with rosemary syrup

PREP + COOK TIME **2 HOURS 40 MINUTES + STANDING** | SERVES **12**

Semolina is a coarsely ground flour milled from the hardest part (endosperm) of the durum wheat grain and is commonly used in making gnocchi, pasta, and couscous. Although it is not gluten-free, it is high in potassium, digested more slowly than white flour, and is fibre-rich. Here it imparts a rich, nutty flavour to the cake, kept extra moist with the aromatic syrup.

2 large oranges (600g)

1 tsp baking powder

6 eggs

1 cup (220g) caster sugar

1 cup (150g) fine semolina

1¼ cups (150g) almond meal (ground almonds)

1½ tsp finely chopped fresh rosemary

rosemary syrup

2 large oranges (600g)

½ cup (110g) caster sugar

½ cup (125ml) water

1½ tbsp lemon juice

2 tbsp orange-flavoured liqueur

3 sprigs fresh rosemary

1 Place the unpeeled oranges in a medium saucepan, cover with cold water; bring to the boil. Cook, covered, for 1½ hours or until the oranges are tender; drain. Cool.

2 Preheat oven to 180°C (160°C fan/350°F/Gas 4). Grease a deep 22cm round cake pan; line the bottom and side with baking paper.

3 Trim and discard the ends from the oranges. Halve the oranges; discard seeds. Process the orange, including rind, with the baking powder until the mixture is pulpy. Transfer to a large bowl.

4 Process the eggs and sugar for 5 minutes or until thick and creamy. Stir the egg mixture into the orange mixture. Fold in the semolina, almond meal, and rosemary. Spread the mixture into the lined pan.

5 Bake the cake for 1 hour or until a skewer inserted into the centre comes out clean; cover loosely with foil halfway during baking if over browning. Leave cake to cool in the pan for 45 minutes. Transfer, top-side up, onto a cake plate.

6 Meanwhile, to make the rosemary syrup, remove the rind from one orange in long thin strips with a zester. Using a vegetable peeler, peel a long continuous strip of rind from the remaining orange. Place the sugar, water, and lemon juice in a small saucepan over a low heat; stir, without boiling, until the sugar dissolves. Add the long strip of rind, bring to the boil; boil for 5 minutes or until the syrup thickens. Remove from the heat; stir in the liqueur, rosemary, and thin strips of orange rind.

7 Spoon the hot syrup over the warm cake. Serve the cake warm or at room temperature.

TIP

If you don't have a zester, simply peel the rind into wide strips with a vegetable peeler, then cut into thin strips.

Pistachio, walnut, and chocolate baklava

PREP + COOK TIME **1 HOUR 10 MINUTES + STANDING** | MAKES **36**

Baklava is probably the most recognizable of all sweet Greek pastries, with its origins dating back to the Ottoman Empire. It is a rich, sticky dessert made of layers of filo pasty filled with chopped nuts and held together with either a sugar syrup or honey. We've added dark chocolate to our version of baklava, to up the decadent level of this sweet treat.

12 sheets filo pastry

120g unsalted butter, melted

2 tbsp finely chopped pistachios

pistachio and walnut filling

1½ cups (210g) pistachios

2 cups (200g) walnuts

200g dark (semi-sweet) chocolate, coarsely chopped

⅓ cup (75g) caster sugar

2 tsp ground cinnamon

1½ tbsp finely grated orange rind

honey syrup

1 medium orange (240g)

1½ cups (330g) caster sugar

1½ cups (375ml) water

½ cup (175g) honey

⅓ cup (80ml) orange juice

1 Preheat oven to 190°C (170°C fan/375°F/Gas 5). Grease a 22cm x 40cm x 2.5cm oven tray; line with baking paper.

2 For the pistachio and walnut filling, spread the pistachios and walnuts on an oven tray; roast in a 180°C (160°C fan/350°F/Gas 4) oven for 5 minutes or until the nuts are golden brown (stir nuts once during roasting for even cooking). Cool completely. Process the nuts with the remaining ingredients until finely chopped.

3 Layer three pastry sheets, brushing each with a little of the butter. Keep the remaining sheets covered with baking paper and topped with a clean, damp tea towel to prevent drying out. Spread a quarter of the filling over the pastry, leaving a 3cm border along both long sides. Starting at one long side, roll up the pastry to form a log. Place the log on the oven tray, brush with butter. Repeat with the remaining pastry, butter, and filling.

4 Bake the baklava for 20 minutes or until golden.

5 Meanwhile, make the honey syrup. Remove rind from the orange in long thin strips with a zester. Stir the rind, sugar, water, and honey in a small saucepan, over a medium heat, without boiling, until the sugar dissolves. Bring to a simmer; cook for 10 minutes or until thickened slightly. Stir in the orange juice.

6 Stand the baklava on the tray for 5 minutes to cool slightly. Using a small sharp knife, cut each log, on the diagonal, into nine 2cm wide pieces in the tray. Pour the hot syrup over the baklava; stand for 3 hours or until the syrup is absorbed. Serve topped with chopped pistachios.

TIP

Serve with Greek yogurt, sprinkled with finely grated or thinly sliced orange rind, if you like.

Raspberry ricotta cheesecake

PREP + COOK TIME **1 HOUR 30 MINUTES + REFRIGERATION AND COOLING** | SERVES **8**

The inclusion of ricotta in this cheesecake makes the filling lighter than the traditional cream-cheese based dessert. Amaretti are Italian biscuits made from almonds, which legend has it were created to welcome a visiting cardinal to the town of Saronno. The recipe for the biscuits was supposedly kept as a family secret over many generations.

200g amaretti biscuits

2 tbsp caster sugar

75g unsalted butter, melted

125g raspberries (see tips)

2 tbsp icing sugar

2 tbsp water

125g raspberries, extra

2 tsp icing sugar, extra

raspberry ricotta filling

500g cream cheese

300g ricotta

1 cup (220g) caster sugar

1/3 cup (80ml) milk

3 eggs

125g raspberries

1 Grease a 20cm (8in) springform pan; line the bottom and side with baking paper.

2 Process the biscuits and caster sugar until fine crumbs form. With the motor operating, gradually add the butter until well combined. Press the biscuit mixture over the bottom of the lined pan using the back of a spoon. Place the pan on an oven tray; refrigerate for 30 minutes.

3 Preheat oven to 150°C (130°C fan/300°F/Gas 2).

4 Make the raspberry ricotta filling. Process the cheeses, sugar, and milk until smooth. Add the eggs; process until combined. Transfer the mixture to a large bowl; fold in the raspberries. Pour the filling into the lined pan.

5 Bake for 50 minutes or until the cheesecake is cooked around the edge and slightly wobbly in the middle. Turn oven off; cool the cheesecake in the oven for 1 hour with the door ajar. (The top of the cheesecake may crack slightly on cooling.) Refrigerate for 4 hours or overnight, until firm.

6 Process the raspberries, icing sugar, and water until pureed. Strain through a sieve into a small bowl. Spread some puree over the cheesecake, top with extra raspberries; dust with extra icing sugar. Serve with the remaining puree.

TIPS

• You can use thawed frozen raspberries for the raspberry sauce, if you like.

• Depending on the design of the springform pan, clip the base in upside down so the base is level; this makes it easier to remove the cheesecake.

Fruit compote

Fruit compote is great paired with yogurt or muesli, or try stirring it into your porridge to liven up your breakfast. To turn a compote into a desert, add a crumble topping and bake, or serve with ice-cream and waffles.

Pear, cardamom, and ginger

VEGAN | PREP + COOK TIME **45 MINUTES** | SERVES **4**

Place 4 (1kg) cored and thickly sliced packham pears in a medium saucepan with 1 cup (250ml) water, 2 teaspoons of freshly grated ginger, 6 bruised cardamom pods, 1 cinnamon stick, and 1 tablespoon of lemon juice; bring to the boil. Reduce heat; simmer, partially covered, for 25 minutes, stirring occasionally, or until the liquid has reduced slightly and the pears are tender. Serve warm or chilled.

Vanilla-roasted nectarines and peaches

VEGAN | PREP TIME **35 MINUTES** | SERVES **4**

Preheat oven to 220°C (200°C fan/425°F/Gas 7). Grease a medium ovenproof dish. Halve and remove the stones from 3 medium (510g) yellow nectarines and 3 medium (450g) yellow peaches; place in the dish. Split a vanilla bean lengthways; scrape seeds from the halves, using the tip of a knife. Add the vanilla bean and seeds to the dish with 2 tablespoons of pure maple syrup, 2 x 4cm strips of lemon rind, 1 tablespoon of lemon juice, and a pinch of sea salt flakes; turn the fruit to coat it. Arrange the fruit in a single layer, cut-side up. Bake the fruit for 20 minutes or until the fruit is tender but still holds its shape. Serve warm or chilled.

Apple, rhubarb, and goji

VEGAN | PREP TIME **25 MINUTES** | SERVES **4**

Place $1/2$ cup fresh orange juice and 2 tablespoons of rice malt syrup in a medium saucepan over a low heat; cook, stirring, until the syrup melts. Add 2 large (400g) coarsely chopped Pink Lady apples, a 4cm wide strip of orange rind, the seeds scraped from half a vanilla bean and the pod; simmer, covered, for 5 minutes. Add 1 bunch (500g) trimmed, coarsely chopped rhubarb and 2 tablespoons of goji berries; simmer gently, covered, for 10 minutes or until the fruit is tender and still holding its shape. Serve warm or chilled.

Plum, raspberry, and rosemary

VEGAN | PREP TIME **25 MINUTES** | SERVES **4**

Halve and remove the stones from 5 blood plums (450g); cut each half into thirds. Place the plums in a large saucepan with $1/4$ cup (60ml) water, 1 tablespoon of lemon juice, 1 cinnamon stick and 2 sprigs fresh rosemary; bring to the boil. Reduce heat; simmer, covered, for 5 minutes. Uncover; simmer, for a further 5 minutes or until the plums are just tender. Stir in $1/2$ cup raspberries (65g) and 2 teaspoons of norbu (monk fruit sugar) until the norbu dissolves. Remove from the heat.

CLOCKWISE from top left

Melt 'n' mix strawberry yogurt cake

PREP + COOK TIME **1 HOUR 15 MINUTES + COOLING** | SERVES **8**

Mediterranean desserts sometimes have the reputation of being overly fussy (though meals are often concluded simply with fresh fruits, some sharp cheese, and a night-time tipple). Here we have a moist and nutty cake that requires no more than one bowl to prepare, so there is no excuse not to indulge in a freshly-baked cake for dessert.

2$\frac{1}{2}$ cups (375g) self-raising flour

250g strawberries, coarsely chopped

1 cup (220g) golden caster sugar

1 tsp vanilla bean paste

2 eggs, lightly beaten

1 cup (280g) Greek yogurt

125g unsalted butter, melted

$\frac{1}{2}$ cup (40g) flaked almonds

icing sugar, for dusting

1 cup (280g) Greek yogurt, extra

macerated strawberries

250g strawberries, sliced

1 tbsp lemon juice

1 tbsp golden caster sugar

1 Preheat oven to 180°C (160°C fan/350°F/Gas 4). Grease a 22cm springform pan; line the bottom and side with baking paper.

2 Sift the flour into a large bowl; stir in the strawberries, sugar, vanilla paste, egg, yogurt, and butter until just combined. Spoon the mixture into the pan; smooth the surface. Sprinkle with almonds.

3 Bake the cake for 50 minutes or until a skewer inserted into the centre comes out clean; cover loosely with foil halfway through baking if the almonds are over browning. Leave cake in the pan for 10 minutes. Release the ring; transfer the cake to a wire rack to cool.

4 Meanwhile, make the macerated strawberries. Combine the ingredients in a small bowl; stand for 20 minutes.

5 Top the cake with the macerated strawberries and dust with icing sugar; serve with the extra yogurt.

TIP

The cake and macerated strawberries are best made on the day of serving.

Honey and vanilla custard pots with filo crunch

PREP + COOK TIME **40 MINUTES + REFRIGERATION AND COOLING** | SERVES **4**

Filo comes from the Greek word for leaf, referring to its thin, paper-like texture. It is mainly used for making pastries, both sweet and savoury. Layering many sheets of filo, brushed with olive oil or butter, results in a very crumbly, delicate structure when baked. Here the filo is used as a crunchy element to contrast with the smooth, silky honey custard.

¹/₄ cup (90g) honey

2 cups (500ml) milk

1 vanilla bean, split lengthways

2 tbsp custard powder

1 tbsp brown sugar

1 sheet filo pastry

olive oil cooking spray

2 tbsp finely chopped unsalted pistachios

1 tbsp honey, extra, warmed

4 medium fresh figs (240g), quartered (see tip)

1 Place honey, milk, and vanilla bean in a medium saucepan over a medium heat; bring to a simmer.

2 Whisk the custard powder and sugar in a medium heatproof bowl until combined. Gradually whisk the warm milk mixture into the custard mixture; return to the pan. Bring to the boil, whisking constantly, until the mixture boils and thickens. Discard the vanilla bean.

3 Pour the mixture into four 1-cup (250ml) dishes. Refrigerate for 2 hours or until chilled and firm.

4 Meanwhile, preheat oven to 180°C (160°C fan/350°F/Gas 4). Line an oven tray with baking paper.

5 Place a pastry sheet on a work surface; spray with oil. Sprinkle two-thirds of the pistachios over the pastry. Fold the pastry in half crossways; brush with extra honey, sprinkle with the remaining pistachios. Bake for 8 minutes or until golden and crisp; cool. Break into pieces.

6 Serve the custards topped with the figs and filo crunch, drizzled with a little more honey, if you like.

TIP

Swap the figs for ripe strawberries, raspberries, or your favourite stone fruit, if preferred.

Dark chocolate and ricotta mousse

PREP + COOK TIME **20 MINUTES + COOLING** | SERVES **6**

The hard and fast rule for chocolate is that the higher the percentage of cocoa, the better it is for you. Quality dark chocolate is rich in fibre and iron, and is a great source of antioxidants. While you shouldn't be eating large quantities of chocolate in one sitting, as it is high in sugar and calories, a bit of dark chocolate in your diet is a great sweet treat.

$^{1}/_{4}$ cup (90g) honey

1 tbsp dutch-processed cocoa

2 tbsp water

$^{1}/_{2}$ tsp vanilla extract

200g dark chocolate (70% cocoa), coarsely chopped

8 fresh dates (160g), pitted

$^{1}/_{2}$ cup (125ml) milk

2 cups (480g) soft ricotta

2 tbsp pomegranate seeds (see tips)

2 tbsp chopped pistachios

1 Stir the honey, cocoa, water, and vanilla extract in a small saucepan over a medium heat; bring to the boil. Cool.

2 Place the chocolate in a small heatproof bowl over a small saucepan of simmering water (don't let the water touch the base of the bowl); stir until melted and smooth.

3 Process the dates and milk until the dates are finely chopped. Add the ricotta; process until smooth. Add the melted chocolate; process until well combined.

4 Spoon the mousse evenly into six $^{3}/_{4}$ cup (180ml) serving glasses. Spoon the cocoa syrup on the mousse; top with the pomegranate seeds and pistachios.

TIP

Fresh pomegranate seeds are sometimes found in the fridge section of supermarkets or good greengrocers. If they're not available, see page 131 for instructions on how to remove them from the fruit. Alternatively, top each serving with fresh cherries instead.

Roasted fig and yogurt ice-cream

PREP + COOK TIME **45 MINUTES + COOLING AND FREEZING** | SERVES **8**

This is more of a frozen yogurt, so it is less creamy than traditional ice-cream. Lower in fat than cream, this also makes it a healthier choice. Greek yogurt is rich in probiotics, which are live bacteria and yeasts that are good for your health, especially your digestive system. The probiotic found in yogurt is known as lactobacillus, which helps breaks down lactose.

6 large ripe figs (480g), torn in half

$^3/_4$ cup (165g) brown sugar

2 tsp finely grated orange rind

$^1/_3$ cup (80ml) freshly squeezed orange juice

3 cups (840g) Greek yogurt

$^2/_3$ cup (160g) crème fraîche

$^1/_3$ cup (115g) honey, plus extra to serve

6 ripe figs (240g), extra, halved

1 Preheat oven to 220°C (200°C fan/425°F/Gas 7). Grease and line an oven tray with baking paper.

2 Place the figs, sugar, orange rind, and orange juice on the tray; toss to combine. Spread the figs on the lined tray in one layer, cut-side up; roast for 15 minutes or until tender and bubbling. Cool for 10 minutes.

3 Grease a 2-litre (8-cup) loaf pan; line the bottom and sides with baking paper; extending the paper 5cm (2in) over the long sides.

4 Combine the yogurt, crème fraîche, and honey in a large bowl; gently fold in the caramelized figs and the fig roasting juices. Spoon the mixture into the lined pan. Freeze for 4 hours or until partially frozen.

5 Remove from freezer. Coarsely chop the mixture; place in a large food processor bowl, pulse to break up the ice crystals. Return to the pan. Freeze for 4 hours or until firm.

6 Serve ice-cream topped with the extra figs; drizzle with extra honey.

TIPS

- Stand the ice-cream at room temperature for 10 minutes to soften slightly before serving.
- If you have an ice-cream machine, this mixture can be churned following the manufacturer's instructions.
- Store leftover ice-cream in the freezer for up to 1 month.

Citrus yogurt cups

PREP + COOK TIME **45 MINUTES** | SERVES **4**

In the dark, cold months of winter, the only bright spot is the copious ripe, juicy citrus fruits that come into season. While it is well known that citrus are an excellent source of vitamin C, which helps boost your immune system in the cold and flu season, they also possess other health benefits, such as the antioxidant-rich red grapefruit, which helps to lower cholesterol.

1 vanilla bean

$1/3$ cup (75g) caster sugar

$1/2$ cup (125ml) water

6 wide strips orange rind (see tip)

1 tbsp orange juice

2 medium mandarins (200g), peeled, sliced horizontally

1 medium ruby grapefruit (350g), peeled, segmented

3 cups (840g) Greek yogurt

small fresh mint leaves, to serve

1 Split the vanilla bean in half lengthways; scrape seeds into a small saucepan. Add the vanilla pod, sugar, water, and orange rind to pan; bring to the boil. Reduce heat to low; cook for 6 minutes or until the syrup has thickened slightly. Cool. Discard the vanilla pod; stir in the orange juice.

2 Combine the mandarin and grapefruit slices and sugar syrup in a medium bowl.

3 Spoon the yogurt into four $1^1/_4$ cup (310ml) serving glasses. Top with the citrus mixture and mint.

TIPS

• For orange strips, use a vegetable peeler to peel wide strips and avoid taking off too much of the white pith with the rind, as it is bitter.
• The syrup can be made 4 hours ahead and combined with the citrus; refrigerate until needed.

Honey-baked peaches and grapes with sweet ricotta

PREP + COOK TIME **40 MINUTES** | SERVES **4**

There is no more straightforward dessert than baked fruit, where their bright, sweet flavours are amplified to become a delicious warming dish, which is healthy to boot. Accompanied here with a sweetened ricotta, you could also serve the fruit with ice-cream, crème fraîche, or creamy Greek yogurt. Or use the fruit and syrup as a topper for a plain cake.

4 large peaches (880g), stones removed, quartered (see tips)

400g red grapes, halved, seeds removed

1 tbsp honey

4 sprigs fresh thyme, plus extra to serve

1¹/₂ cups (360g) firm ricotta

2 tbsp caster sugar

¹/₂ tsp finely grated orange rind, plus extra to serve

1   Preheat oven to 200°C (180°C fan/400°F/Gas 6). Line an oven tray with baking paper.

2   Place the peaches and grapes on the tray; drizzle with honey and top with thyme. Bake for 25 minutes or until tender and syrupy.

3   Meanwhile, process the ricotta, sugar, and orange rind until smooth.

4   Serve the baked fruit and any cooking juices with the ricotta mixture, topped with the extra orange rind and fresh thyme.

TIPS

- Use plums instead of peaches, if you like.
- This dish can be served for brunch or dessert. It also travels well, so is a great picnic basket addition. Pack the ricotta and fruit separately; keep the ricotta cold.

Baked ricotta pudding with orange syrup and cherries

PREP + COOK TIME **1 HOUR + COOLING AND REFRIGERATION** | SERVES **4**

Honey has been collected by humans from ancient times, and in the absence of sugar was used as a sweetener in many traditional desserts in the Mediterranean region. The earliest recording of honey harvesting is in an 8,000-year-old cave painting in Valencia, Spain, which depicts two figures using a ladder to gather the sweet liquid from high bee hives.

900g fresh ricotta

4 eggs

$^1/_2$ cup (175g) honey

$^3/_4$ tsp ground cinnamon

2 tsp finely grated orange rind

100g fresh cherries, seeded

2 tbsp coarsely chopped pistachios, to serve

orange syrup

1 large orange (300g)

$^1/_2$ cup (175g) honey

100ml water

1 cinnamon stick

$^1/_2$ tsp fresh thyme leaves

1   Preheat oven to 180°C (160°C fan/350°F/Gas 4). Grease a 4-cup (1 litre) ovenproof dish.

2   Process the ricotta, eggs, honey, cinnamon, and orange rind until smooth. Pour the mixture evenly into the dish.

3   Bake the pudding for 30 minutes or until the centre is just firm to touch. Cool to room temperature. Refrigerate for 1 hour or until cold.

4   Meanwhile, make the orange syrup. Finely grate rind from the orange; squeeze out the juice, you will need $^1/_4$ cup (60ml) orange juice. Combine the rind, juice, and remaining ingredients in a small saucepan; bring to the boil. Reduce heat to low; cook for 10 minutes or until syrupy. Refrigerate for 1 hour or until cold.

5   Serve the pudding topped with the cherries, orange syrup, and pistachios.

Conversion chart

A note on Australian measures

- One Australian metric measuring cup holds approximately 250ml.

- One Australian metric tablespoon holds 20ml.

- One Australian metric teaspoon holds 5ml.

- The difference between one country's measuring cups and another's is within a two- or three-teaspoon variance, and should not affect your cooking results.

- North America, New Zealand, and the United Kingdom use a 15ml tablespoon.

Using measures in this book

- All cup and spoon measurements are level.

- The most accurate way of measuring dry ingredients is to weigh them.

- When measuring liquids, use a clear glass or plastic jug with metric markings.

- We use large eggs with an average weight of 60g.

Dry measures

metric	imperial
15g	$^1/_2$oz
30g	1oz
60g	2oz
90g	3oz
125g	4oz ($^1/_4$lb)
155g	5oz
185g	6oz
220g	7oz
250g	8oz ($^1/_2$lb)
280g	9oz
315g	10oz
345g	11oz
375g	12oz ($^3/_4$lb)
410g	13oz
440g	14oz
470g	15oz
500g	16oz (1lb)
750g	24oz (1$^1/_2$lb)
1kg	32oz (2lb)

Liquid measures

metric	imperial
30ml	1 fluid oz
60ml	2 fluid oz
100ml	3 fluid oz
125ml	4 fluid oz
150ml	5 fluid oz
190ml	6 fluid oz
250ml	8 fluid oz
300ml	10 fluid oz
500ml	16 fluid oz
600ml	20 fluid oz
1000ml (1 litre)	1$^3/_4$ pints

Length measures

metric	imperial
3mm	$^1/_8$in
6mm	$^1/_4$in
1cm	$^1/_2$in
2cm	$^3/_4$in
2.5cm	1in
5cm	2in
6cm	2$^1/_2$in
8cm	3in
10cm	4in
13cm	5in
15cm	6in
18cm	7in
20cm	8in
22cm	9in
25cm	10in
28cm	11in
30cm	12in (1ft)

Oven temperatures

The oven temperatures in this book are for conventional ovens; if you have a fan-forced oven, decrease the temperature by 10–20 degrees.

	°C (Celsius)	°F (Fahrenheit)
Very slow	120	250
Slow	150	300
Moderately slow	160	325
Moderate	180	350
Moderately hot	200	400
Hot	220	425
Very hot	240	475

Index

Acknowledgments

DK would like to thank Sophia Young, Simone Aquilina, Amanda Chebatte, and Georgia Moore for their assistance in making this book, and Lyndi Cohen for the introductory text.

The Australian Women's Weekly Test Kitchen in Sydney, Australia has developed, tested and photographed the recipes in this book.